TEACH *Well,*
LIVE *Well*

*To our daughter Maya Sierra, you have brought
tremendous joy into our lives.
We love you!*

TEACH *Well,* LIVE *Well*

Strategies
for
Success

John **LUCKNER**

Suzanne **RUDOLPH**

CORWIN
A SAGE Company

For information:

Corwin
A SAGE Company
2455 Teller Road
Thousand Oaks, California 91320
(800) 233-9936
Fax: (800) 417-2466
www.corwinpress.com

SAGE India Pvt. Ltd.
B 1/I 1 Mohan Cooperative
    Industrial Area
Mathura Road, New Delhi 110 044
India

SAGE Ltd.
1 Oliver's Yard
55 City Road
London EC1Y 1SP
United Kingdom

SAGE Asia-Pacific Pte. Ltd.
33 Pekin Street #02-01
Far East Square
Singapore 048763

Printed in the United States of America.

Library of Congress Cataloging-in-Publication Data

Luckner, John L.
Teach well, live well : strategies for success / John Luckner, Suzanne Rudolph.
      p. cm.
Includes bibliographical references and index.
ISBN 978-1-4129-5575-1 (cloth)
ISBN 978-1-4129-5576-8 (pbk.)
    1. Effective teaching. 2. Teachers—Professional relationships. I. Rudolph, Suzanne. II. Title.

LB1025.3.L83 2009
371.102—dc22   2008056063

This book is printed on acid-free paper.

09   10   11   12   13   10   9   8   7   6   5   4   3   2   1

Acquisitions Editor:	Carol Chambers Collins
Editorial Assistant:	Brett Ory
Production Editor:	Eric Garner
Copy Editor:	Paula L. Fleming
Typesetter:	C&M Digitals (P) Ltd.
Proofreader:	Carole Quandt
Indexer:	Terri Corry
Cover Designer:	Karine Hovsepian

Contents

Acknowledgments

Corwin gratefully acknowledges the following reviewers for their contributions:

Roxie R. Ahlbrecht, NBCT
Second-grade classroom
 teacher/mathematics
 teacher leader
Robert Frost Elementary
Sioux Falls, SD

Dr. Rodger J. Beatty
Associate dean, faculty of
 education
Brock University
St. Catharines, ON, Canada

Cynthia A. Givens
Director, The Education Station
 (at-risk program)
Central High School
Cheyenne, WY

Jane Hunn
Science teacher
Tippecanoe Valley Middle
 School
Akron, IN

Jude A. Huntz
Adult education coordinator
St. Michael the Archangel
 Catholic Church and
 School
Leawood, KS

Sharon Jefferies
M.Ed., N.B.C.T.
Elementary teacher, Lakeville
 Elementary
Orlando, FL

About the Authors

John Luckner, EdD, is a professor in the School of Special Education at the University of Northern Colorado. He has worked as a classroom teacher, teacher trainer, researcher, and author for the past three decades. His primary professional interests include teacher preparation, language and literacy development, and collaboration. He is the coauthor of four books and one test and the author of several textbook chapters, and has written more than 75 juried journal articles.

Suzanne Rudolph, EdD, is a licensed clinical psychologist, certified personal and professional life coach, and clinical member of the American Association for Marriage and Family Therapy. She has assisted others with making important changes in their lives for the past 16 years and has a private practice in northern Colorado where she lives with her husband and daughter.

Introduction

Each of us wants to experience an enriched professional life and a satisfying personal life. Teaching can provide the sense of purpose and real meaning that no other profession can offer. Teaching allows us to achieve the satisfaction of knowing that we positively influence the lives of others, while simultaneously creating a quality life for ourselves.

Teaching is society's most important occupation. It is the only profession dedicated to making the world a better place for future generations by focusing energy and attention on our most precious resources—children and youth. And teachers have the opportunity to influence the lives of individuals regardless of their ethnicity, cultural background, socioeconomic status, or ability level. As such, teaching is the one profession that makes all other professions possible.

While teaching is an essential profession, it is also one that is currently experiencing a great deal of external pressure. The demands of our current service- and knowledge-driven global economy have placed intense pressure on our educational system to produce better results. Teachers are required to educate more students, with more challenges, to higher levels of learning than at any time in the history of public education. Higher educational standards, greater accountability for all students, and a more diverse student population are significantly changing the working conditions of teachers. In addition, the world we live in has become more complex. Our lives are changing faster than at any time in human history. Information is expanding at an unprecedented rate, and the technology that allows us to store, organize, access, and exchange the ever-growing explosion of information changes almost daily.

More than any time in the history of the United States, a quality education—one that helps students acquire the important skills, knowledge, and values necessary to be a success in tomorrow's world—is essential. With an understanding that the workplaces of the present and the future demand a new kind of worker, schools are being asked to produce literate, self-determined, emotionally intelligent, and socially skilled lifelong learners. Certainly, this is a formidable task. Yet it is a worthy challenge. For it is the processes, as well as the outcomes, of teaching and learning that profoundly affect the quality of our individual and collective lives.

Teach Well, Live Well: Strategies for Success is an essential resource for both new and veteran teachers. It provides valuable information about how to (a) prepare properly, (b) teach effectively, (c) collaborate with others, (d) deal successfully with the changing demands of the job, and (e) identify ways for teachers to take care of themselves so they can stay vibrant and productive and lead balanced lives.

1

Preparing Properly

Have a Great Year and Career

Nothing great has ever been achieved without enthusiasm.

—Ralph Waldo Emerson (1803–1882),
American author and philosopher

You are going to have a great year because the work you do is important and meaningful. You are going to have a great school year because

- you will interact with students who exhibit liveliness, curiosity, freshness, openness, spirit, and independence.
- you will feel pleased when you have taught a lesson well and students demonstrate their enthusiasm and understanding through their responses to questions or the projects they develop.
- you will have the opportunity continually to learn more and to share that knowledge with students.
- you will see the glow of understanding on students' faces.
- you will have the chance to be creative—to develop lessons, facilitate discussions, and create projects.
- you will connect with a student whom many others have given up on.

- you will have the opportunity to be a quasi-actor, performing on stage for an audience of students.
- you will be part of a team that works together to provide services for students and families.

You also will want to tell yourself, "It's going to be a great year," because healthy, optimistic thinking leads to improved performance and increased job satisfaction (Seligman, 2002). Similarly, striving to maintain a positive state of mind, a belief in personal control, and an optimistic view of the future will not only help you adapt to stressful events more successfully but will also help protect your health (Taylor, Kemeny, Reed, Bower, & Gruenewald, 2000). Consequently, you want to develop a mind-set of personal control and optimism about yourself, your students, your colleagues, and the great year you are going to have because these traits will help you to manage the ebb and flow of everyday life and to cope more effectively with challenging events (Seligman & Csikszentmihalyi, 2000).

Now keep in mind that having a great school year doesn't mean that everything is going to go smoothly and that you are not going to experience challenges, setbacks, and negative events. Research consistently has documented educators' concerns about discipline, large class or caseload sizes, excessive paperwork, diminishing resources, and challenging student behavior. Teaching today is a more demanding occupation than in the past. Increasingly, teachers are expected to compensate for the shifts in society and family that affect children and youth. Teachers are required to comply with legal mandates, respond to public demands and criticism, and teach more complex content to a higher level of mastery. At the same time, the student population is becoming more diverse across a host of variables, such as linguistic, cultural, and socioeconomic factors.

As you can imagine, teaching, like all other forms of work, will never be devoid of stressful conditions or interactions. Such occurrences are part of living and working in the 21st century. To meet these daily challenges, you will need to be mentally, physically, and emotionally prepared. You will want to cultivate a mind-set of optimism and find ways to maximize your achievements and to savor your successes. Simultaneously, you will want to remind yourself, and your colleagues, of the positive influence you have on the lives of the students with whom you work and their families. And most importantly, you will want to determine personally appropriate ways to take care of yourself and to find ways to continue to learn and to grow so you can stay vibrant, effective, and productive.

Bottom Line

✓ Recent research published by the National Opinion Research Center (NORC; Smith, 2007) indicates that satisfaction in one's job is positively related to general happiness. NORC also reported that in comparison to all occupations, teachers ranked sixth in overall job satisfaction, scoring higher than many other well-known professions (e.g., physicians, lawyers, police officers, nurses, accountants, psychologists, authors, and engineers).

✓ Working in the field of education provides you with an opportunity to do essential work. It offers a focus for your life; grants you an identity; and gives you an arena for self-expression, contribution, socialization, and personal growth. Yet like all professions, teaching presents challenges as well as a unique set of pressures, which are very different from other occupations. To cope effectively with the pressures intrinsic to the field of education, you will need to take proactive steps; you must regularly find ways to recharge, apply your talents, and continue to learn and develop. Equally importantly, you must take the time to create a personal life that is enjoyable and satisfying.

Maintain Perspective

The purpose of life is happiness. Happiness is determined more by the state of one's mind than by one's external conditions, circumstances, or events—at least once one's basic survival needs are met. Happiness can be achieved through the systematic training of our hearts and minds, through reshaping our attitudes and outlook. The key to happiness is in our hands.

—Dalai Lama & Howard Cutler,
The Art of Happiness at Work (2003)

The teaching profession presents a unique set of stressors that can challenge your ability to maintain perspective. The daily requirements of teaching effectively and being professional while interacting with members of the school community provide numerous opportunities to experience stress. Common sources of stress include interactions with difficult students or parents, an insensitive administrator, school politics, an excessive workload, poor work environment, conflict with a coworker, unrealistic expectations of yourself, fear of failure, and negative thinking. In addition, the rhythm of the school year and the fluctuating pace of work demands may at times leave you feeling drained and exhausted. Although you may feel that you do not have control over these stressful factors, you do have influence over your own attitude and responses to the challenges you're facing in both your personal and professional life. Consider for a moment, why is it that when two people are blindsided by events at school, such as a last-minute change in the grade they were planning to teach or having to deal with an upset parent, one person may cope relatively well, while the other may feel stressed out and miserable? All things being equal, perspective plays a huge role in how we cope with stress. Although at times, we do not have control over our circumstances, we do have the ability to choose our own attitudes and behaviors. People who maintain an optimistic perspective when faced with adversity tend to be more resilient and to cope more effectively with stress.

According to Seligman (2002), optimism and hope are associated with better work performance and health. Optimistic people tend to view their problems as transient and situation-specific. They perceive themselves as having some control. Pessimists, on the other hand, perceive their troubles as long lasting and uncontrollable. Based on these differences in perspective, optimistic people are more likely than pessimists to engage in behaviors that improve their situations or lives. Consequently, pessimistic or negative thinking can undermine our sense of confidence and our ability to cope and impair our performance. In other words, our perspectives and the stories that we tell ourselves and others about the events that occur in our lives influence the way we feel, the choices we make, and our behavior. Below are some ways to maintain perspective in your life:

- One way to increase optimism and emotional well-being is through the practice of mindfulness. Mindfulness is the ability to be aware of and conscious of your thoughts, feelings, and behaviors in the present moment in a nonreactive way, rather than responding to events on automatic pilot or out of old habits (Fralick, 2007). When you are having a strong emotional reaction, be it anger, sadness, fear, or worry, take a few moments to breathe and to reflect on what you are telling yourself. Notice your automatic thoughts. Are you reacting to current circumstances based on past experiences? Are you being critical of yourself, or are you overly focused on a negative outcome? Then evaluate the situation or circumstances from a more balanced perspective. How can you look at this situation differently? Are you ignoring evidence in yourself or in the situation that you can use to change your perspective? What choice can you make now? Notice how your feelings shift as you seek evidence that helps you to develop a more balanced perspective.

- On a daily and weekly basis, look for evidence that supports your belief that teaching is a valuable, rewarding profession. People who view their work as meaningful, as making a contribution and having a higher purpose, are more satisfied in both their work and their personal life (Dalai Lama & Cutler, 2003). Start your day with a positive outlook. Find ways to remind yourself why you enjoy teaching and the students you teach every day. Consider writing down your intentions about your day in a journal; in the evening, reflect on and write about three things that went well in your day.

- Make a habit of seeing setbacks and mistakes as opportunities for learning. Remember that you are not only a teacher but you are also a lifelong learner. So when things don't go well, learn from them rather than judging yourself.

- Appreciate what you have rather than dwelling on what you don't have. Make a list of the things for which you are grateful. Review and add to this list often.

- You are responsible for your own well-being and for taking care of your health. If you find yourself feeling overwhelmed on a frequent basis, see the sections in Chapter 6 titled "Balance Your Personal and Professional Life" and "Set and Maintain Boundaries" to learn more about what you can do to take care of yourself.

Bottom Line

✓ When you hit a bump in the road of life, it's your interpretation of events that will have a significant influence on the way you feel and the choices you make. You have the power to choose your own attitude and response to the circumstances in your life.

✓ On a daily basis, if you look for ways to love teaching, you will find them.

Learn the Policies and Procedures

The best preparation for tomorrow is to do today's work superbly well.

—Sir William Osler (1849–1919),
"founding father" of modern medicine

The start of the school year arrives fast and furious. While it is exciting and fun to think about the students you will teach, the colleagues with whom you will work, and the content on which you will focus, it is important to make time before the school year begins to look over the schoolwide policies and procedures. Most of this information is available in a faculty handbook, online, or in handouts given to you at meetings. Get in the habit of saving all policy and procedure documents in one place (e.g., loose-leaf notebook, file folder in a filing cabinet). Also, read the policies so you have a good sense of what the routine procedures are and what course of action you are expected to take when nonroutine situations arise. Following are a few general suggestions:

- Prior to signing your contract, review it to make sure the salary is correct, to identify any additional duties expected of you, and to document the dates of employment. Make a copy for yourself.
- Contact the human resources department to go over your health plan and benefits.
- Acquire a school calendar that includes school days, vacations, staff development days, parent-teacher conferences, and special events. Post it someplace where you can view it easily and transfer the information into your planning calendar.
- Find out about access to the building and the room in which you will be teaching. Will administration provide you with keys to the building and the room? How early can you arrive at school? How late can you stay? Can you work in the building on weekends?
- Ask about lesson plans. Must a specific format be used? Do they have to be submitted to an administrator for review? If so, when? Can they be handwritten in a weekly planner, or does the administration want you to use a computer-based system?
- Become familiar with the school's discipline procedures. What is the suggested sequence for dealing with a problem when it initially occurs? How should you document reoccurring problems?

Who can you talk with if you need help with a student or a group of students?

- See if a formal mentoring program is available. If so, how is it structured? If not, can the administration suggest someone with whom you can work?
- Determine how sick days or personal days are handled. Whom do you call, and when can you call?

Listed below are more nitty-gritty issues that require your attention. If at all possible, try to get answers before school starts because once students arrive, you will be busy planning and delivering lessons.

- Meeting and dismissing students at the beginning and end of the day
- Taking and reporting attendance
- Bell system or changing classes
- Making copies
- Requesting audiovisual equipment
- Referring a student for counseling
- Referring a student for special education testing
- Time for collaboration
- Requesting additional equipment (e.g., desks, chairs, tables)
- Requesting supplies and materials (e.g., books, paper, pencils)
- Requesting repairs in the room
- Sick or hurt student
- Food in the classroom
- Assessment (e.g., state tests, standardized, informal, documentation)
- Grading
- Report cards
- Fire drills
- Lockdown drills—inside threat
- Lockdown drills—outside threat
- Shelter in place drills (e.g., hazardous material or chemical incident outside building)
- Tornado drill
- Earthquake procedures
- Homework policies
- Use of the library
- Parent/guardian communication and conference procedures
- Lunch schedule and procedures
- What to do if you suspect child abuse
- What to do if you suspect a student is using illegal drugs

- Use of classroom volunteers
- Field trips
- Dress code for teachers
- Tardiness
- Excessive absences
- Textbook distribution
- Detention
- Emergency safety procedures
- Class parties
- Celebrating holidays
- Student medication
- Suspected cheating or plagiarism
- Assessment and grading
- Dress code for students
- Hall passes
- Use of cell phones

Bottom Line

✓ Each school district, as well as each school within the district, is unique in how it operates. You need to understand big-picture issues, such as the district mission statement and school initiatives, as well as detailed information, such as the policies and procedures to which students and faculty are expected to adhere. While certainly not the most stimulating learning you will undertake, becoming familiar with the faculty and student handbooks and finding out about each of the issues listed above will be beneficial for you and the students you teach.

Be Proactive

If you don't have time to do it right, you must have time to do it over.

—Anonymous

Successful people in all walks of life are good planners. On the personal level, it is important to plan because research suggests that individuals who are happy are (a) engaged in work that is meaningful and satisfying, (b) live in a caring and supportive network of interpersonal relationships, and (c) pursue and make progress toward intentionally chosen goals that are congruent with personal values and resources (Argyle, 1999). Consequently, we want to consciously use our time, energy, and resources to be happy and to lead a meaningful life.

We only have 168 hours (10,080 minutes) to live each week. When we deduct the time needed for sleep and to complete chores, it becomes evident that making the time to plan and prioritize is important on a regular basis. In today's radically changing world, so many stimuli are competing for our attention. And because life is full of pressures and stresses, it is easy to slip into the pattern of taking action without thought. Yet without personal goals and making a habit of frequently examining progress toward meeting those goals, it is difficult to achieve the quality of life that we each deserve. Here are a few questions to consider from time to time:

- Am I an interesting person?
- Am I having fun in life?
- Am I satisfied with my health and vitality?
- Do I like the person I have become?
- Am I satisfied with my relationships?

On the professional level, it is important to plan to help reduce the stress in your life. The rapid pace of the events that occur in most classrooms, sometimes as many as 200 interchanges per hour, is the underlying reason why planning plays such an essential role in stress reduction. While it can be creative and exhilarating to "wing it," and you will need to ad-lib on occasion, teaching is a lot easier when you are familiar with the content you want to teach, have organized the materials you need, and have anticipated problems before they occur. Interactions are better, lessons run more smoothly, class time is used more efficiently, and you are more open to "teachable moments" when you have invested time in developing plans.

To teach effectively, you will need to develop long-range, unit, weekly, and daily plans. Begin long-range planning by examining the content standards and the suggested scope and sequence, so you are clear on what content you are expected to teach and what outcomes students are expected to demonstrate. Examine the school calendar and decide approximately how much time you have available to devote to each topic of study.

Unit planning involves deciding the collection of lessons that will address a single topic, theme, or skill (e.g., math—single-digit division, reading—informational texts, history—the Civil Rights movement). Units vary in length, ranging from a few lessons spread out over the course of a week to many lessons that span more than a month. When planning units that are aligned with the content standards, you will want to do the following:

1. Identify what you want students to know and be able to do by the end of the unit.

2. Determine by what evidence students will demonstrate that they have mastered the content.

3. Select the core activities through which the content and skills can be taught and learned.

4. Consider the resources (e.g., instructional materials, people, places) you will use.

5. Divide the unit into lessons.

Weekly plans are often dictated by the master school schedule, which includes the starting and ending time of each day, established times for lunch, curriculum time allotments, and designated times for specials such as gym and computer lab. Write your weekly plans in pencil or use a word processing program so you can make changes as you go along. Also, develop a system that allows you to make quick notes to yourself about what needs to be reviewed or retaught or what was not taught because of a special activity or occasion (e.g., assembly, current event discussion).

Lesson plans vary in appearance and detail. Generally they contain a list of steps or procedures that the lesson will follow. The process of writing down the purpose, procedures, and needed resources can help clarify them in your mind. The lesson plan can also serve as a guide for visitors. Finally, you may be able to use the lesson plan at a later time to remind you of what was done and how effective it actually was.

Bottom Line

✓ The path to personal fulfillment is paved by your individual goals, plans for meeting those goals, and taking action. Make time to plan and reflect so that you can create a meaningful life for yourself.

✓ Develop a picture of what you want students to achieve over the course of the year or the semester by examining the content standards, the curriculum materials, and the units of study with which you will be working.

✓ Create your short-term assessments and end-of-unit assessments prior to planning your weekly and daily lessons. Doing so will help you focus on the standards you want to meet and the content you want students to demonstrate mastery of.

✓ When planning, take into consideration the students who learn content quickly, the average learners, and the students who need additional practice and/or review. How will you enrich the fast learners and provide additional learning opportunities for those who need them?

✓ Toward the end of the week, arrange a block of uninterrupted time to write your plans for the following week. Consider the resources you will need, how you will engage students in the topic, the in-class and homework assignments that students will complete, and how you will provide closure to each lesson.

Design the Physical Environment

If people knew how hard I had to work to gain my mastery, it wouldn't seem wonderful at all.

—Michelangelo (1475–1564),
Italian Renaissance artist

The physical layout of the classroom should reflect your teaching style as well as your personality. A few questions to consider are these:

- Where do you want your desk to be?
- Where will you keep your personal valuables (e.g., purse, wallet, keys)?
- Where will you keep all your teaching materials and records?
- Do you want students to have individual desks or work at tables?
- If they have individual desks, do you want them in rows, small clusters of four desks that face each other, or in a U shape?
- How will you get students in position for whole-class instruction?
- What types of media equipment (e.g., whiteboard, overhead projector, Smartboard, LCD display, CD player) do you like to use, and is it available for you to use? How will you get the equipment in place when conducting whole-class instruction?

- Do you want a place for small-group instruction?
- Will you have a computer workstation for yourself? Will you have one for students to use? Where are the electrical outlets?
- Where will students store their belongings?
- Do you want to set up a reading center and/or a learning center?
- Where will students submit and store their completed work?

When arranging the room, be certain that you can monitor the total classroom environment from all the key locations and that the arrangement of the room allows you to see every student and each student can hear and see every other student.

Consider accessibility issues. You will want to be able to get to each student. You'll want students to be able to get to each other so that they can work together on assignments. You'll want students to be able to get to materials. You'll want to avoid having obstacles (e.g., desks, bookshelves, wastebaskets) near high-traffic areas, such as the door, pencil sharpener, and storage areas, and you'll want to make sure that power cords are out of the way or taped to the floor so no one trips over them.

The walls and bulletin boards add a great deal to the visual attractiveness of the classroom. When deciding how to use the available space, consider two purposes—decorative and informational. A balance should exist. Examples for decorative appeal include the following:

- Photos of students
- Student work samples
- Calendar and holiday themes
- Students' birthdays in chronological order
- Book jackets
- Positive messages/motivational sayings
- Posters
- Self-portraits or silhouettes
- Pennants
- Flag
- Comics and cartoons

Informational examples include these:

- Class rules
- Daily schedule
- Class job chart
- Content standards
- Maps
- Lunch menu
- Bell schedule

- School map
- Weather chart
- Handwriting chart
- Word walls
- School news
- Pictures of current events
- Homophone, antonym, and synonym charts
- Graphic organizers of current units of study
- Time lines
- Photos related to current units of study
- List of steps for completing a procedure (e.g., editing a writing assignment, dividing fractions, conducting an experiment)

Bottom Line

✓ Setting up the classroom requires you to take time to think about how you want to conduct business. You will need to decide how to arrange your personal space, the places where learning will occur, the furniture and materials, and the flow of traffic.

✓ You and the students you teach will spend a large portion of every week in the classroom. Think about how you can make it an aesthetically pleasing and efficient environment that stimulates learning.

✓ Consider your strengths and personal interests when deciding how to decorate the room. If you are artistic and enjoy decorating, make the time to share your talent and create a visually attractive environment that reflects your personality. If you are not creative and don't enjoy decorating, purchase prepackaged materials and posters or trace pictures on the walls using an opaque projector. Also, consider asking a paraprofessional or a classroom volunteer to help.

Establish Routines

Decide what you want, decide what you are willing to exchange for it. Establish your priorities and go to work.

—H. L. Hunt (1889–1974),
American oil tycoon

For each of us, the demands of daily living, such as eating, sleeping, travel to and from work, teaching, housework, running errands, and finding time to exercise and relax, can be draining. Individuals who fail to develop routines for many of these daily activities add unneeded pressure to their lives. Routines are tasks or procedures that are generally performed in a similar manner each time. Routines help each of us to be efficient—doing work as quickly and easily as possible—and to be effective—getting the greatest return on our efforts. Establishing routines for yourself and the students you teach will help you (1) save time and effort; (2) free up your mind to think creatively; and (3) create order, reduce stress, and help students succeed in your classroom.

Routines for You

Consider developing routines for the following daily tasks:

- Laying out clothes for the next day
- Making and eating breakfast
- Packing healthy snacks and lunch
- Storing your wallet, purse, keys, and glasses
- Opening, sorting, and storing mail
- Answering e-mail/phone calls

Make your professional life easier by developing routines. The following are examples of work-related routines and suggestions for addressing each task:

- *Arrival at school*—Try to arrive early enough to make sure that you have reviewed your schedule and plans and pulled together the materials and equipment you are going to need for the day.
- *Student information*—Create a folder for each student and use it to store and access information about students.
- *Photocopying*—Make your copies a few days or a week in advance. Make extra copies to be certain you have enough.
- *Supplies*—Keep frequently used materials (e.g., pens, pencils, passes, forms) handy and keep a supply in a safe place.
- *Equipment*—Examine each piece of equipment, such as overhead projectors, LCD, CD players, and video players, to make sure it works before you plan to use it for a lesson.
- *Record keeping*—Keep student contact, attendance, and grading information in a grade book, file cabinet, or computer jump drive that you can easily access.
- *Grading*—Develop a rubric or grading sheet when you create an assignment. Record students' grades weekly.

- *Documentation*—Keep a pencil, notepad, and calendar by the phone and computer and record calls and e-mails.
- *Storing materials*—Use differently colored binders for different subjects (e.g., reading is blue, math is red), or if you teach the same subject, use the differently colored binders for different classes (e.g., green for seventh-grade math, yellow for eighth-grade math). Use storage boxes for units of instruction. Put the materials, activities, bulletin boards, and lesson plans in the box.

Routines for Students

Every teacher runs his or her classroom differently. Help students succeed in your classroom by teaching them the procedures you want them to use. In addition, you will want to let them know what things (e.g., your desk, file cabinets) belong to you and are off-limits to them unless they have your permission.

In general, it is best to be very explicit when teaching routines. The younger the students, the more detailed you will need to be. Use a five-step sequence to teach a routine:

1. Name the routine, tell the steps, and then demonstrate appropriate behavior.

2. Check to make sure students understand the steps.

3. Have students practice the routine.

4. Observe students as they practice the routine and provide positive feedback.

5. Reteach if necessary.

Below is a list of events that occur daily in most classrooms. Review the list and identify the events for which you would like to develop a routine. Then, envision how you would like the routine to occur and sequence the steps you will teach students.

- Entering the classroom
- Leaving the classroom
- Opening exercises
- Taking attendance
- Taking lunch count
- Using the restroom
- Getting a drink of water
- Sharpening pencils

- Getting/distributing paper and other supplies
- Asking the teacher for help
- Using free time
- Using reference materials
- Using the computer
- Writing headings on work to be submitted
- Transitioning between lessons
- Submitting completed classwork
- Submitting completed homework
- Gathering work for absent students
- Submitting work when returning from being absent
- Behaving appropriately when the teacher leaves the room
- Greeting visitors
- Going to the nurse
- Conducting fire drills
- Reacting to emergencies

Bottom Line

✓ There is always too much to do and too little time to get everything done. Establishing and implementing routines in your personal and professional life will help you be more efficient and have a little more time to do the things you enjoy and/or want to do.

✓ In well-run classes, students know the schedule and what they are expected to do. They feel secure in the predictability of the environment, and they know that staying on task and learning are the highest priorities. Simultaneously, teachers waste little time answering questions about daily procedures, such as sharpening pencils, getting a drink of water, and turning in homework.

Develop General Rules
of Conduct for Students

Failure is an event, not a person.

—Zig Ziglar,
American motivational speaker and author

Effective teachers establish well-organized classrooms where students feel safe and able to work attentively at their learning tasks without unnecessary distractions and interruptions. To create such an environment, you will need to prevent inappropriate student behavior, respond to a student whose behavior is unacceptable, and reinforce students who demonstrate appropriate behavior.

Establishing Classroom Rules

In a well-managed classroom, students know that good behavior is important and that mutual respect and cooperation are expected. Establishing and implementing a set of classroom rules provides students with guidelines for what is acceptable and what is not. You can develop the set of classroom rules on your own, or you can do it as a class activity, eliciting rules from students and then making sure that the rules selected are reasonable and that they address the primary issues of classroom behavior (e.g., talking, moving around the room, how to treat each other, personal responsibility). Consider the following strategies when developing rules:

- Limit the number of rules to five or six.
- Spend time introducing the rules (preferably on the first day of class). Explain each rule; demonstrate an example of appropriate behavior and an example of inappropriate behavior related to that specific rule.
- State classroom rules positively (e.g., "Work quietly," rather than, "Do not disturb other students.").
- Post a copy of the rules in a prominent place so students can easily be reminded of them. For younger students, you may want to include pictures.
- Send a letter with the classroom rules home, so parents or guardians can reinforce the expectation of appropriate behavior.
- Review the list of rules several times during the first couple weeks of school.

Following are some examples of rules for elementary students:

1. Follow school rules.

2. Treat other people with respect.

3. Raise your hand to speak or leave your seat.

4. Take turns communicating.

5. Try to complete all your work.

6. Keep your work and work area neat.

Following are examples of rules for middle school and high school students:

1. Obey all school rules.

2. Bring your materials to class every day.

3. Be in your seat when the bell rings.

4. Raise your hand to speak or if you need help with an assignment.

5. Be respectful of others and their property.

Enforcing Rules

Students will test you to see if the rules are going to be enforced and to find out what the consequences will be. They will also misbehave from time to time, and they will have momentary lapses in judgment. Be clear—enforcing rules is part of your job.

When you create the rules, it will be necessary also to decide what the consequences will be when a student breaks a rule. Develop the consequences that will occur if the rule is not followed and hold students accountable for their behavior by enforcing the consequences consistently. Of course, consequences will vary depending on the age of the students you teach. Sample consequences in order of severity are as follows:

- Reminder
- Warning
- Talking with the student privately
- Moving a student's seat
- Loss of a privilege (e.g., recess, time after lunch, attending a class party)
- Phone call home
- Time out
- Short detention
- Writing a reflective essay on the causes and effect of the rule and developing a plan of action for avoiding the problem in the future
- Development of a behavioral contract

- Referral to an administrator or the counselor
- Parent/guardian conference
- Longer detention

Preventing Behavior Problems

In addition to establishing routines and developing, teaching, and enforcing rules, you also can try to prevent behavior problems by monitoring students and providing ongoing feedback. Position yourself so that you can consistently visually scan the classroom. Move around the room during lessons, involve as many students as possible in discussions and learning activities, and give eye contact and/or move into the physical proximity of students who have difficulty staying on-task.

Transitioning from one subject to another or from one room to another place occurs frequently throughout the school day. If not managed properly, those occurrences provide ample opportunities for wasting time, student misbehavior, and/or negative student-teacher interactions. Consequently, it is important to develop and then teach students your rules of transitioning. In addition, you will want to get in the habit of providing students with a cue about upcoming transitions (e.g., "Finish your work. We are going to start reading in three minutes."). For younger students, consider using a countdown game, whereby everyone needs to have everything put away or everyone needs to have his or her materials and be standing quietly in line by the time you finish counting down from 15 to 1. Praise students for their appropriate behavior.

Provide clear and consistent linguistic and nonverbal messages when commenting on behavior that needs to change. Try to phrase your remarks positively rather than negatively. For example, instead of saying, "Stop fooling around and do your work," say, "Time to get to work." Simultaneously, it is important to praise the class as a group when they are on task and when they have worked well together. When possible, it is best to praise individual students in private. You can also provide individual and/or group reinforcers. Examples include the following:

- *Social reinforcers*—Verbal praise, working with a friend, playing with a classmate, being an activity leader, free time, positive phone call home
- *Tangible reinforcers*—Stickers, certificates, toys, games, fast-food coupons, pencils, pens, tickets to movies, baseball cards, drop-the-lowest-grade coupon, no-homework pass

- *Activity reinforcers*—Playing a game, popcorn party, computer time, reading a book or magazine, class trip, listening to music, homework exemption, watching a movie
- *Primary reinforcers*—Piece of candy, soft drink, piece of fruit (prior to giving out food as a reinforcer, check with a school administrator to find out the school and district policy)

Managing Student Behavior: What Else Can You Do?

- A positive class atmosphere and well-planned, organized lessons are the best ways to avoid behavior problems.
- Learn and use students' names.
- Students are more motivated to learn when they interact with adults whom they perceive as interested in them, wanting them to succeed, concerned about their needs, and trying to understand their perspectives.
- Give explicit instructions for activities and independent or group work you want students to complete. Check to make sure they know the steps of what needs to be done prior to letting them start their work.
- Research reported by Lane, Pierson, and Givner (2003) suggests that five social skills are essential for school success for K–12 students: (1) following directions, (2) attending to instructions, (3) controlling one's temper in conflict situations with peers, (4) controlling conflict situations with adults, and (5) responding appropriately to physical aggression from peers. These skills should be explicitly taught to students and reinforced regularly. Students who experience difficulty developing these skills may benefit from additional training from the school counselor or a special education teacher.
- Integrate students' interests in food, sports, music, and other aspects of culture into the examples you use to clarify concepts and to teach important vocabulary.
- Save your voice by using gestures to communicate to students what you want. For example, tap your watch to let them know that they are wasting time, tap on students' desks to let them know they are off-task, and use the thumbs-up when they are working well.
- Acquire an American Sign Language book and teach students the signs for words and phrases such as stop, sit down, pay attention, work, quiet, finished, and line up.

- Have designated activities (e.g., brainteaser book, puzzle magazine, computer programs, or special projects) for students to do if they complete their seatwork early.

- Losing your temper, raising your voice, and yelling at students may momentarily change their behavior, but more often than not, it impairs relationships with students. Find a way to calm yourself and to control your reaction before letting the situation escalate into something you feel terrible about later.

- The time-out is an effective tool when appropriately used for situations where students are being mildly disruptive. Ask misbehaving students to move to the outskirts of the activity. For more severe misbehavior, students can be sent to an out-of-class time-out. Time-outs should be used for only brief periods.

- Avoid punishing the entire class for the misbehavior of one or two students.

- Hold class meetings occasionally to describe and talk about some negative and/or positive behaviors you have observed. Class meetings are also a good time to introduce new procedures, such as how to work in a recently set up learning center.

- Praise is highly effective and easy to deliver. Use descriptive praise rather than global praise. Examples of global praise are "Good job," and "Your math worksheets were very good." Examples of descriptive praise are "I am impressed with the way you put away your books and lined up for lunch so quickly and quietly," and "Your story is well written. It has an interesting beginning and the characters are nicely developed."

- Never grab, pinch, or hit students. You don't want to model the use of physical response as an acceptable way to deal with stress.

- While some behavior problems are the result of organic issues, such as hyperactivity, most misbehavior occurs for one of two reasons: (1) to get something, such as attention, a privilege, or an object or (2) to avoid something, such as schoolwork or interacting with someone. Determining the function of a student's misbehavior can help you develop effective behavior change programs. Also, some students will act out because they are frustrated about being unable to complete the assigned work. See the section in Chapter 3 titled "Differentiate Instruction" for some ideas about adjusting the difficulty level of assignments.

- Keep an up-to-date file listing the date, problem behavior, and consequence for students who demonstrate behavior concerns. You can share the file with the student, parents, counselor, and administration if necessary.

- Monitor yourself to make sure that your personal prejudices are not affecting how you treat students. If you determine that you may subconsciously dislike a student based on past experiences or deep-seated beliefs, talk to a friend or a trusted colleague.
- A mantra related to dealing with behavior problems is "Be calm, be firm, be kind, be consistent."

Bottom Line

✓ Check district and school policies and procedures for dealing with behavior problems.

✓ Students make better choices about their behavior when they know what is expected of them. Developing, reviewing, rehearsing, and enforcing classroom rules positively influences student behavior.

✓ Students are going to misbehave from time to time. You will deal with these misbehaviors effectively one day and not as effectively the next day. Try not to take student misbehavior personally and try not to hold yourself to perfectionist standards. You did the best you could at the time the situation occurred. Learn from you successes and your less-than-successful incidents. Try to be reflective about what occurred, adopt a problem-solving approach, and be better prepared the next time students misbehave.

✓ Talk to your colleagues, mentor, and administrators about the way they deal with student misbehavior if you find it interfering with student learning.

Prepare for the First Day of School

I learned that life is not a dress rehearsal, and that today is the only guarantee you get. I learned to look at all the good in the world and to try and give some of it back because I believed in it completely.

—Anna Quindlen,
American journalist and novelist

Teaching is one of the only professions that has a fresh start each and every year. New students, new colleagues, new content, new mandates—how exciting, how stressful! Yes, it is stimulating to be able to begin a new school year. It is also a bit overwhelming.

Because the first day of school sets the tone for the year, it is important that you plan appropriately. Your Day 1 goals will include welcoming students; establishing a positive environment for learning; and communicating to students your hopes and expectations, as well as the rules, routines, and structure of the classroom.

Getting the year off to a good start begins long before the students enter the classroom. Be sure to read the previous sections "Be Proactive," "Design the Physical Environment," "Establish Routines," and "Develop General Rules of Conduct for Students." Each section contains information critical for starting the year on the right foot. The following are some additional actions you can undertake to set the stage for a wonderful first day, which in turn lays the foundation for a successful academic year:

- Dress well. Look professional. Take into consideration how the other professionals at school dress, the weather, the ages of the students you teach, and your own personal preferences.
- Don't drink too much coffee or too many caffeinated drinks.
- Acknowledge how you feel. Being nervous, excited, and worried about how the day will go is all part of starting fresh. Honor how you feel; smile and act as confident as you possibly can.
- Be organized and prepared. Develop plans for what you think students will be able to do and then add a couple of additional activities just in case they get done more quickly than you expect. Have materials and activities ready.
- Arrive early. Get there early enough to have all your materials and activities laid out and ready to go. Plan on colleagues, parents, or students stopping by to say hello.
- Determine how seats will be assigned—prearranged (e.g., alphabetical order, boy-girl order) or self-selection? Are there students with special needs and/or medical conditions? If so, consider if specific locations in the classroom would be beneficial or unfavorable for them (e.g., you don't want to seat a student with attention deficit/hyperactivity disorder near the door or windows).
- Develop a seating chart. Draw a diagram of the seating arrangement you decided to use and make a rectangle for each desk in the class. Write each student's name in the designated seat.

- Develop a plan for learning and using students' names. You can begin by taking attendance, checking how students pronounce their names, and finding out if students have a nickname or a shortened form of their name they prefer. The seating chart, name tags, name plates, mounting digital photos of each student on a bulletin board seating chart, and/or playing name games are all useful in learning students' names.
- Welcome students at the door. Share a smile and an inviting statement, such as "Good morning, I'm glad you are here," with each student.
- Introduce yourself. Have a name tag with your name on it in the hallway by the classroom door; also have your name written on the board. Share some information about yourself (e.g., how you say your last name, what you want students to call you, how long you have been teaching, how long you have been teaching at this school, where you grew up, if you have family and/or pets). Keep it short and upbeat.
- Introduce the schedule, the routines, and the rules. Have a daily schedule on the board or on the bulletin board available for students to examine. Review when daily activities occur (e.g., lunch, recess for young students, changing classes for older students). Walk around and point out the different sections of the classroom. Describe the purpose of each section of the room; the materials in that section; and the routines for entering, exiting, and using each section of the room. Spend time discussing the routines and either develop or review the classroom rules. Describe the consequences for breaking the rules.
- Organize a get-acquainted, icebreaker type of activity. In the Resources section at the back of this book, several texts with icebreaker activities are listed. Choose an activity that is age-appropriate, is not too difficult, and doesn't take very long to complete. Try to find a comfortable way for students to interact with each other, as well as to share something about themselves. Examples include human treasure hunts, personal time lines, interest inventories, and interview and introduce a partner exercises.
- Orient students to the school. With young students, you may want to tour the school together, showing them the important places (e.g., bathrooms, water fountains, lunchroom, main office, gym, nurse's office, bus drop-off and pickup) and introducing them to some of the important people (e.g., principal, vice principal, counselor, secretary, nurse, custodian). For older

students, you may want to give each student a map and review it together.

- Provide a preview of the curriculum, the projects, and/or the field trips. Most of us have grown up enjoying the coming attractions of television shows, radio programs, and movies. Provide students with a sneak peek of the interesting topics they will be studying this year, trips they will be taking, and unique experiences they will have.

- Conduct a lesson. Read and discuss a story, talk about current events, give students a writing prompt, develop a web of prior knowledge about an upcoming unit of study, or use one of the activities from the section titled "Incorporate Activities" in Chapter 3 to engage students' minds and to get a sense of how students function.

- Distribute welcome packets to be taken home to parents/ guardians. If you or school staff have not previously sent a note, newsletter, or welcome packet to the family before school starts, then you may want to send one home the first day. Items to consider including are an introduction letter that tells a little about yourself and your experience in education, contact information, a list of supplies the child will need, homework policy, grading policy, a request for parent/guardian support, examples of volunteer opportunities in the school and/or the classroom, a calendar of school events, and forms that need to be completed.

- Discuss emergency and safety procedures. If time permits on Day 1, then talk about fire drills and evacuation routes. If time is tight, then talk about this topic later in the week. Younger students will need to practice prior to the first fire drill. You should also make sure that you know the evacuation route and where you are supposed to bring your students. Make sure all of your students exit the classroom before you close the door to the classroom and that you have access to your attendance book so you can make sure all students are present.

- Explain the grading policy. This is another topic that you may or may not get to the first day, but it needs to be addressed within the first few days of the school year. Will you use a point system? How often will you have tests? What types of tests do you like to give—multiple-choice or essay? Does homework count toward the final grade? How important is class participation? Do you prefer projects to tests? Will students be expected to develop portfolios? Providing answers to these types of questions will decrease students' anxiety and set the tone for what you expect of students.

- Wrap up. Leave time at the end of class and/or the school day to restate that you are excited about the new school year. Tell students again that you are looking forward to getting to know them and to watching them learn and work together cooperatively. Remind them about the routines and the rules and talk about the schedule for the next day.

Bottom Line

✓ The start of a good school year begins before the first day of school, and a well-planned first day keeps the momentum going in the right direction.

✓ Spend part of the first day and the first week teaching, modeling, rehearsing, monitoring, and reteaching the rules and procedures you want students to use.

✓ Create a positive first impression with the students you teach and the colleagues with whom you work by demonstrating a positive attitude, high expectations, classroom management proficiency, and good teaching skills right from the start of the school year.

2

Teaching Effectively Part I

Reaching Every Student to Maximize Learning

Understand and Appreciate Students

I long to accomplish a great and noble task, but it is my chief duty to accomplish small tasks as if they were great and noble.

—Helen Keller (1880–1968),
American author and activist

Life is neither as simple nor as predictable as it was in the past. A variety of complex social issues impact the students we teach, as well as the schools in which we work. Society is challenged by family distress, the influence of illegal drugs and alcoholism, poverty, child and spousal neglect and abuse, increased crime and violence, and teen pregnancy to name a few commonly cited problems. Additionally, students are more diverse—culturally, economically, emotionally, behaviorally, physically, and intellectually—than ever before. Simultaneously, when students complete school, they must be prepared to compete in a rapidly changing world and a global economy, which requires ever increasing levels of intrapersonal, interpersonal, and content knowledge and skills.

Like it or not, we are affected by most of the changes occurring in society. To prepare the next generation for the world they will live in, as well as to maintain perspective about our societal problems, it is valuable to remind ourselves about the universal needs of human beings and how these needs influence behavior. Several authors (e.g., Blocher, Heppner, & Johnston, 2001; Ormrod, 2008; Ryan & Deci, 2000) suggest that in addition to our basic physiological needs (e.g., oxygen, water, food, warmth, exercise, and rest) and safety needs (i.e., to feel safe and secure), humans have three growth needs:

1. *Relatedness*—We are social creatures; people of all ages have a fundamental need to feel socially connected and to secure the love and respect of others.

2. *Competence*—We need to believe that we can deal effectively with our environment. Our self-worth is enhanced by achieving success on a regular basis or by avoiding failure. Consequently, people often avoid tasks they expect to do poorly and/or make excuses to justify their poor performance.

3. *Self-determination*—We want to have a sense of autonomy regarding the things we do and the directions our lives take.

Maintaining an awareness of human needs can help us understand why the student who is hungry has a hard time paying attention, why the student who recently was yelled at in class by another teacher doesn't want to participate in an activity, why a student whose parents are going through a nasty divorce is preoccupied with her peers, why the student who doesn't think he is a good reader refuses to read out loud in front of his classmates, and why the student who is told to write an essay on Sir Francis Drake is resistant—but excited and willing to develop a PowerPoint presentation on the contributions of James Cook. If we understand that students' behavior is often a continuous attempt to satisfy one or more of their basic needs—and if we try to identify, celebrate, and nurture students' strengths, capacities, knowledge, and skills, rather than focusing on their problems and failures—we increase the likelihood of establishing environments that enable students to use their existing strengths to master important aspects of their lives, solve problems, and achieve their aspirations.

Motivation

"Motivation is an internal state that arouses us to action, pushes us in certain directions, and keeps us engaged in certain activities"

(Ormrod, 2008, p. 489). In general, students are motivated if they find the goal attractive and if they believe they can attain the goal. In contrast, students may lack motivation because (1) they don't see the value of learning the subject or developing a specific skill, (2) they believe that they are going to fail, or (3) they believe that the satisfaction of obtaining the goal is not worth the effort required to attain it.

Motivation can vary in intensity and duration across a host of factors, such as the subject, the unit of study, the type of learning experiences, the teacher, and the chemistry of the students in the class or group. To increase motivation, we want to help students understand the value of obtaining specific goals (e.g., learning about immigration or how to write a business letter); help them see that the goal is obtainable; and, when appropriate, ease the effort required on their part by breaking content down into manageable units that build toward the successful attainment of the larger goal. Additional suggestions for encouraging motivation are the following:

- Ensure that the lessons are at the appropriate difficulty level. Content that is too easy will cause students to lose interest. Conversely, students will not persist or maintain a positive attitude about content that is too difficult. Please see the section in Chapter 3 titled "Differentiate Instruction" for ideas about adjusting the content of lessons for students.
- Help students see the importance and relevance of learning the material or acquiring the skill. Relate it to their current interests, local or national problems, or its future usefulness.
- Model enthusiasm and interest in the topic of study.
- Teach students how to set goals and monitor their progress. Challenge students to improve on their previous best performances.
- Make the content interesting. Use students' names, interests, backgrounds, and concerns in examples and questions. Use a variety of instructional strategies (e.g., discussions, debates, drama, cooperative learning, projects, problem solving, simulations, journal writing, learning centers, interactive technology).
- Help students recognize the quality of their work. Provide positive feedback and praise to students to acknowledge their achievement and/or persistence of effort.

Poverty

According to the U.S. Census Bureau (2007b), 36.5 million Americans lived in poverty in 2006. Unfortunately, many families in poverty have one or more members who have full-time, year-round work, yet they are not paid wages high enough to get out of debt. The majority of those individuals work in the service or retail trade occupations.

Poverty has potentially harmful effects on all aspects of a student's life, including health, family interaction, emotional well-being, cognitive development, and school performance (Park, Turnbull, & Turnbull, 2002). Students who live in poverty often come to school hungry, tired, and worried about their basic needs. Frequently, families in poverty lack appropriate medical care, live in substandard housing, and have poor diets. Consequently, many students who live in poverty enter school with fewer experiences (e.g., visiting a library, museum, and firehouse) and school-readiness skills (e.g., recognition of colors and shapes, knowledge of numbers and letters, and ability to follow directions) than their peers. As a result, they may have great difficulty closing the gap academically. The following are suggestions for working with students who live in poverty, adapted from Holloway (2003):

- Create a learning environment that is positive and safe.
- Be aware of signs of economic hardship, such as wearing the same clothes every day and not having school supplies. Communicate your observations with administrators and social workers so that community resources for students and families in poverty can be accessed.
- Help students and their families complete the appropriate forms, such as those necessary for school breakfast and lunch.
- Identify and comment on the strengths that students demonstrate. When appropriate, encourage them to become involved in extracurricular activities aligned with their talents.
- Consider the suggestions provided in the section in this chapter titled "Include Adaptations for Students With Special Needs" and the section in Chapter 3 titled "Differentiate Instruction" when planning instruction.

Multiple Intelligences

Students acquire knowledge and skills in different ways. Gardner (1999) suggests that each of us has preferences about how we learn and how we demonstrate what we have learned. Gardner suggests that human cognitive competence consists of eight domains of intellect. All normal individuals possess potential for developing each domain of intellect, but individuals differ in the degree and extent to which development occurs, depending on (a) environmental factors,

(b) personality factors, (c) motivational factors, (d) cultural factors, and (e) health factors. Each domain of intellect develops independently of the others, but a combination of intellectual functioning is involved in the course of most human activities. Similarly, each of us possesses varying amounts of the eight intelligences, which we combine and use in highly personal ways. Brief explanations of the domains, examples of specific behaviors, and examples of instructional options for each domain are presented in Table 2.1.

Table 2.1   Multiple Intelligences: Domains, Sample Behaviors, and Instructional Options

Logical-mathematical intelligence—Ability to reason logically, especially in mathematics and science

Behavioral indicators:

- o Likes puzzles, both manipulatives and pencil-paper types.
- o Recognizes relationships between and among objects and ideas.
- o Likes to experiment in controlled, orderly ways.
- o Can follow complex chains of reasoning.
- o Can mentally sort, categorize, and order objects and ideas.
- o Likes logical argumentation.
- o Likes step-by-step operations but can shorten the process sometimes by making logical leaps.
- o Likes collections; devises orderly systems for dealing with collections.

Sample instructional options:

- o Create Venn diagrams.
- o Design and conduct an experiment.
- o Produce a time line.
- o Use technology.

Spatial intelligence—Ability to notice details of what one sees and to imagine and manipulate visual objects in one's mind

Behavioral indicators:

- o Likes to build things.
- o Can use the mind to manipulate mental images of objects as if they were in actual time and space.
- o Draws a lot; uses diagrams, sketches, other graphic representations to help explain thinking.
- o Can imagine objects or diagrammatic representations of ideas; see relationships among them; and manipulate or transform these images, either mentally or in the physical world, for a purpose.

(Continued)

(Continued)

- o Can figure out how to do fairly complex things just by observing the process or looking at pictures.
- o Can figure out the process of how something was done by seeing the finished product.
- o Builds elaborate play structures.

Sample instructional options:

- o Create charts, maps, and/or graphs.
- o Develop a multimedia presentation.
- o Create a poster, picture, or sculpture.
- o Perform mental imagery.

Bodily-kinesthetic intelligence—Ability to use one's body skillfully

Behavioral indicators:

- o Seems to learn and express self through conscious use of the body.
- o Likes to touch things.
- o Likes to act out things, showing physically how something works or can be done.
- o Can learn and put together a complex sequence of physical activities with relative ease.
- o Has excellent manual dexterity; can manipulate things that require fine muscle control.
- o Likes to "clown around."
- o Is physically very active but generally in purposeful ways.
- o Is graceful and economical in use of body movements.

Sample instructional options:

- o Role-play or simulate.
- o Design a product.
- o Make a model.
- o Choreograph a dance.

Interpersonal intelligence—Ability to notice subtle aspects of other people's behaviors

Behavioral indicators:

- o Likes and seeks interaction with others.
- o Gets along well with others; is very sociable.
- o Is sensitive to the feelings and moods of others.
- o Can often figure out the motivations and intentions of others.
- o Reads body language well.
- o Able to influence others; is persuasive.
- o Often assumes a leadership role with others.
- o Likes to be helpful or consoling.

Sample instructional options

- o Participate in a group activity.
- o Conduct a service project.
- o Teach others.
- o Plan a field trip.

Intrapersonal intelligence—Awareness of one's own feelings, motives, and desires

Behavioral indicators:

- o Understands own inner feelings, dreams, and ideas.
- o Is individualistic; is not unduly concerned about what others might think of him or her.
- o Knows what he or she wants or needs.
- o Can gain access to inner feelings and express these feelings accurately in a variety of ways (e.g., through actions, language, and creative products).
- o Acts on the basis of knowledge of self.
- o Is independent and generally self-assured.

Sample instructional options:

- o Set and pursue a goal.
- o Keep a journal.
- o Create a rubric to self-assess work.
- o Explore personal values and philosophy.

Linguistic intelligence—Ability to use language effectively

Behavioral indicators:

- o Is very communicative.
- o Likes to read and write.
- o Experiments readily with new vocabulary; learns quickly the right meaning of words and how to use them correctly.
- o Enjoys poetry.
- o Is sensitive and responsive to humor in language.
- o Reasons through language; uses language skillfully to explain things or show how conclusions have been drawn.

Sample instructional options:

- o Participate in a debate.
- o Tell stories.
- o Give a presentation.
- o Conduct interviews.

Musical intelligence—Ability to appreciate, comprehend, and create music

Behavioral indicators:

- o Enjoys listening to music.
- o Shows sensitivity to rhythm and beat, pitch, and qualities of sound.

(Continued)

(Continued)

o Composes music.
o Performs music.

Sample instructional options:

o Write song lyrics.
o Give a presentation with musical accompaniment.
o Compose music.
o Develop a musical collage.

Naturalist intelligence—Ability to recognize patterns in nature and differences among various life-forms and natural objects

Behavioral indicators:

o Enjoys exploring human and natural environments.
o Seeks to understand how things work.
o Recognizes patterns among members of species.
o Looks for opportunities to observe, identify, interact with, or care for plants and/or animals.
o Enjoys using tools, such as microscopes, binoculars, telescopes, and/or computers, to study organisms or systems,

Sample instructional options:

o Collect and categorize data.
o Compare and contrast.
o Describe cycles or patterns.
o Keep a journal of observations.

Bottom Line

✓ Humans are social creatures. We have a fundamental need to feel socially connected and to feel the support and interest of others.

✓ The majority of students in school are "good kids" who come to school to learn and to socialize.

✓ When basic and growth needs are not met, individuals often feel discontented, anxious, or even depressed. The more students can fulfill their needs in school, the more they are likely to apply themselves to what is to be learned.

✓ All students have strengths and preferences for how they learn. If we take the time to recognize and build upon their strengths, students will become more motivated to deal with the demands of school and life.

Attend to the Science of Teaching

Success is the sum of small efforts, repeated day in and day out.

—Robert Collier (1885–1950),
American motivational author

If I am through learning, I am through.

—John Wooden,
American basketball coach

Research indicates that a strong relationship exists between effective teacher behaviors and student learning (e.g., Darling-Hammond, 2000; Good & Brophy, 2007). Examples of teacher behaviors that positively affect student outcomes include planning well, being enthusiastic, being task oriented, using a variety of lesson approaches, asking higher-order questions, using student ideas, and providing students with opportunities to practice content material. Effective teachers adjust their teaching to fit the needs of different students, the age of the students they teach, and the demands of different instructional goals. While no single instructional strategy has been found to be consistently successful with all students, some elements of teacher-centered lessons are effective for helping students master basic skills and concepts. In the first portion of this section, those elements are discussed. In the second segment, other teaching frameworks for promoting learning and the development of higher-order thinking skills are presented.

Elements of Effective Instruction

Secure Student Attention

Prior to beginning any lesson, it is important that you make sure that all students are ready to learn. Move to a place where all students can see you, smile, and make a simple statement, such as "It's time to get started," or "Eyes up here." Wait for students to attend before you begin.

Establish the Purpose of the Lesson by Stating the Objectives

Provide an overview of the lesson and emphasize how the lesson objectives relate to the students' lives. In addition, when possible, try to establish a link between the new information and previously learned material. You can do this by explicitly telling students, "We are going to learn . . . ," or you can start the lesson with an anticipatory setup, such as "What do you know about . . . ?" or by showing students a picture, diagram, or short video related to the topic of study.

Introduce New Material

Present specific points in small, sequential steps and use examples and nonexamples to ensure understanding. Try to maintain a brisk pace and stop to check for understanding by posing questions. You can also assess student understanding by asking students to make predictions, to summarize what has been discussed so far, or to repeat directions or procedures. An ineffective way to check for understanding is to ask, "Are there any questions?" and, after receiving no response, assume that students have learned the material.

Conduct Guided Practice

After you have introduced the new material, or after short segments of your presentation, you will want to provide students with opportunities for active practice. Students' responses to a variety of product questions (i.e., specific answers) and process questions (i.e., explanations of how an answer was found) will help you know if they are ready to proceed or if you need to repeat the key points or provide additional examples. To increase student involvement during guided practice, you can do the following:

- Use choral responding, which requires all students to respond on cue.
- Have students tell the answer to their neighbors.
- Have students record their responses to your questions on individual chalk- or whiteboards; then when you signal, they simultaneously raise their boards to show you their answers.
- Have students write down the answer and then walk around and check their responses.
- Ask students to respond to yes or no questions or true/false questions by placing their thumbs up or down.

Provide Feedback and Correction

During guided practice, you will want to provide students with descriptive and specific feedback. If a student's response is correct and confident, you can inform her that it is correct and ask another question to maintain the momentum of the practice session. If a student answers a question correctly but is hesitant, you will want to provide him with process feedback. Process feedback means that you acknowledge that the answer is correct and then proceed to explain why the answer is right or to describe the process that must be followed to get the right answer. Process feedback is a quick way to reteach the content and to give students another explanation when they are uncertain. When a student has made an error, it is appropriate for you to simplify the question, provide hints that guide the student to the right answer, give the student the process or rule to be used in determining the answer, call on another student, or reteach the material.

Conduct Independent Practice

Independent practice gives students an opportunity to interact with and to demonstrate their understanding of the material. Students will be more engaged during independent practice if you move around the room to monitor their performance and offer prompt feedback. When students submit independent practice work that does not meet your expectations, it should be returned to them to revise and resubmit.

Summarize Main Points and Evaluate Mastery

Before transitioning to the next activity or the next class, summarize the main points of the lesson. Also, conduct assessments of students' mastery of the content on a regular basis so that you use that information to make teaching decisions.

Promote Higher-Level Thinking Skills

On a daily basis, each of us is required to do more than recall information, processes, or procedures. We need to access information, plan responses, organize information, and monitor our performance (Wiggins & McTighe, 2001). These skills are often referred to as higher-level thinking skills. To promote the development and use of higher-level thinking skills in the students you teach, you can (a) organize lessons that include active learning or (b) ask questions that require students to use higher-level thinking skills. Each strategy is briefly discussed below.

Active Learning

Active learning is based on the premise that each of us is inherently active, self-regulating, and intelligently responding to the environment (Iran-Nejad, 1990). To structure active learning experiences that encourage students' planning, action, interaction, problem solving, and reflection, you can refer to the following general framework, suggested by Luckner and Nadler (1997), for creating and planning educational experiences.

- *Simulated experiences*—Students view pictures or movies or role-play simulations of reality (e.g., establish a grocery store in the classroom, conduct a mock trial, role-play a job interview, choose a stock on the stock market and chart its fluctuations).
- *Spectator experiences*—Students observe objects to identify specific behaviors as the basis for subsequent discussion (e.g., go to the police station, go to a meatpacking business, visit a courtroom).
- *Exploratory experiences*—Students are involved in open-ended, real-world activities and settings where they develop an awareness of and personal questions about the subject at hand (e.g., tutor in the classroom of younger children, volunteer at a center for individuals with severe disabilities, interview a professional, shadow a professional).
- *Analytical experiences*—Students are involved in experiences that require the application of theory in real situations, and they learn by a systematic analysis of the setting or by solving problems (e.g., conduct a fundraising event for a class trip, serve on a student advisory council to the principal, develop a cultural awareness or a disability awareness day).
- *Generative experiences*—Students learn by taking part in the creation of products, processes, or relationships (e.g., develop a class newspaper, develop a learning center, write a letter to a senator to change existent legislation, develop a video to demonstrate appropriate recycling procedures).

Additional examples of instructional methods and techniques for promoting active learning include the following:

- *Poster presentations*—Students develop posters on a given topic or issue and then present the information on the poster to a small group of peers and answer questions.
- *Opinionnaire*—Students individually respond to statements listed on a paper related to the current topic of study, such as "Food should not be genetically modified." After responding to

all the statements, students discuss and defend their opinions in small groups or as a class.

- *Debate*—Two students or groups of students present conflicting views to clarify the supporting evidence for and arguments against them.
- *Think-pair-share*—Provide students with a prompt that focuses their thinking, such as a question that requires abstract thought. Have students take a moment to think about their response and then write down an answer. Then, students pair up and talk about their answers. Finally, they discuss the question as a class.
- *Case study research*—Learners observe the implementation of particular practices in an applied setting, then systematically record and analyze the results.
- *Reaction panel*—A panel of individuals reacts to a presentation by an individual or group.
- *Concept maps*—Students construct a diagram that interrelates the major conceptual components of an issue or set of practices.
- *Student-developed questions*—Students write review, comprehension, and challenge questions related to the topic of study. They form teams, which take turns asking the other team a question. Alternatively, you can collect all the questions and ask individual students to answer.
- *Cooperative learning*—Students work in small, mixed-ability groups on a shared learning goal.
- *Gallery tour*—After completing individual or group projects, students place their work on tables or on their desks and tour the room to view the other students' work.

Another action you can take to promote active learning is to use learning contracts. The contract can be developed for an individual student, a group of students, or an entire class. The learning contract serves as a negotiated agreement between you and students that gives students some freedom in acquiring the knowledge and skills that you deem important. You and students discuss the topic of study, establish long- and short-term goals, identify resources, and describe how the students will demonstrate what has been learned. In addition, for some students, you may need to set positive consequences, such as grades or additional opportunities to work independently, for meeting the conditions of the contract. You also may need to establish negative consequences, such as grades or not being able to work independently or with friends, if students do not adhere to the conditions of the contract.

When using contracts, it is important to schedule regular meetings to discuss progress and problems. Following is a sample format for a contract, suggested by Luckner and Nadler (1997):

1. What do you specifically want to learn?

2. What questions do you have regarding this topic?

3. What specific resources can be used to help you learn about this topic?

4. How will you demonstrate what you have learned?

5. When will you demonstrate what you have learned?

Signed: Student
               Teacher
               Date

Questions

Effective teachers ask a lot of questions and attempt to involve students in class discussions. However, more often than not, teachers ask students literal questions—those that require students to recall, name, list, or describe information previously discussed. Deliberate use of inferential questions—those that require students to provide answers that are not explicitly stated in the content and to analyze, compare, and synthesize information—and critical questions—those that ask students to provide personal judgments and reactions to the content and to evaluate and apply the information to other situations—can enrich the learning of students and help them become better thinkers. This topic is discussed in greater detail in the section in Chapter 3 titled "Ask Good Questions."

Include Brain-Based Learning Principles

Increasingly sophisticated medical instruments, such as functional magnetic resonance imaging (fMRI), computerized tomography (CT), positron-emission tomography (PET), and magnetic resonance imaging (MRI), have allowed researchers to gain remarkable knowledge about how the brain develops, changes, learns, and remembers. The following is currently understood:

- The brain is a highly dynamic organ that feeds on stimulation and experience and responds with the development of branching, intertwined neural pathways.

- Learning represents the opening of new or enlarged neural pathways in the brain. The more powerful, significant, or varied the experience or stimuli that initiated the learning, the stronger and more numerous are the synaptic connections, and the better we understand what we learned.
- Learning is the process of constructing meaning. Learning takes place when the brain sorts out patterns, using past experiences to help make sense out of the input it receives. Recognition of patterns facilitates transfer of learning to new situations. Understanding concepts, behaviors, procedures, or skills results from perceiving relationships and linking what is being learned to the individual's past knowledge, current experience, and future needs and aspirations. Hart (1983) identifies six major patterns to which the brain attempts to attach meaning:
  1. Objects (e.g., dog, caterpillar, chairlift, desk, glacier, water fountain)
  2. Actions (e.g., walking, running, swimming, hiking, working on a computer)
  3. Procedures (e.g., getting dressed, showering, paddling a kayak, preparing a report)
  4. Situations (e.g., taking a test, making a presentation, first aid emergency)
  5. Relationships (e.g., me/you, friend/enemy, supervisor/employee, sun/heat)
  6. Systems (e.g., familial, political, educational, legal, weather, organizational)

A variety of brain-compatible instructional practices have been recommended in the literature (e.g., Caine, Caine, McClintic, & Klimek, 2005; Crawford, 2007; Jensen, 2001; Sousa, 2001). Below are some valuable points to take into consideration when planning lessons:

- Research has identified the characteristics of enriched environments, which promote neural development, as contrasted with impoverished environments, which hinder brain growth. Diamond and Hopson (1998) report that enriched environments include the following characteristics:
  - A steady source of positive emotional support
  - A nutritious diet with enough protein, vitamins, minerals, and calories
  - Stimulation of all the senses, though not necessarily all at once
  - An atmosphere free of undue pressure and stress but infused with a degree of pleasurable intensity

o Novel challenges that are neither too easy nor too difficult for students at their stages of development
o Social interaction
o Opportunities to make choices
o A safe atmosphere that promotes exploration and the fun of learning
o Opportunities to be an active participant rather than a passive observer

- New learning creates new neural connections. These connections must be reinforced and strengthened, or they deteriorate. Rehearsal is critical for transferring information from working memory to long-term memory (Ormrod, 2008). Rote rehearsal promotes the remembering of information exactly as presented. Examples include the sequence of the alphabet, spelling, multiplication tables, poetry, and song lyrics. Elaborative rehearsal is required to remember more complex concepts. Learners need to associate the new learning with prior learning to establish sense and meaning. Examples of elaborative rehearsal suggested by Sousa (2001) include the following:

o *Paraphrasing*—Students restate ideas in their own words.
o *Prediction*—After reading a section of a story or a textbook, ask students to predict what events or material will ensue.
o *Questioning*—After reading a textbook or having a discussion, students generate questions about the content that can be used for review at a later time. See the section in Chapter 3 titled "Ask Good Questions" to help students develop questions of varying complexity.
o *Summarizing*—At the end of a story, textbook chapter, or discussion, ask students to summarize the main points of the material. Have them write a paragraph, draw a graphic organizer, or discuss it with one of their classmates.
o *Journal writing*–Ask students to write responses to the following three questions as a closure activity for a lesson.
  1. What did we learn today about . . . (include specific learning objective)?
  2. How does this connect or relate to what we already know about . . . (include topic from past learning)?
  3. How can this help us, or how can we use this information or skill, in the future?

Bottom Line

✓ Life is less predictable and less simple than it once was. In our current global world, reports suggest that information doubles every 72 days (White & Dorman, 2000). Consequently, it is essential that we help students acquire basic skills and concepts, as well as the higher-order thinking skills, they need to succeed in school and when they graduate.

✓ Learning is an active, dynamic process with neural connections constantly changing and being reformatted. Remembering facts, understanding concepts, and developing skills result from linking what is presently being learned to students' past knowledge, current experience, and future needs and aspirations.

✓ The brain with its complex architecture and limitless potential is a highly plastic, constantly changing entity that is powerfully shaped by our experiences. The outer layer can grow if a person lives in stimulating surroundings, but the zone can shrink if the environment is dull or unchallenging. Our job is to establish learning environments that maximize students' brain development.

Apply the Art of Teaching

Kind words can be short and easy to speak, but their echoes are truly endless.

—Mother Teresa (1910–1997), international humanitarian

In addition to developing good lesson plans and conducting well-organized lessons, to be effective, you will need to reach out and invite students to engage in positive relationships with you, their peers, and with the other adults in the school (Stronge, 2002). Research in a variety of fields has demonstrated that technical knowledge is not sufficient to succeed. Rather, a blend of technical knowledge and social-emotional competence separates the star from the average performer (Goleman, 1998). Consequently, an important characteristic of effective teachers is their ability to connect with the students they teach and invite them to do their best.

The importance of having successful relationships with students is explained by the recent research on "social intelligence," which indicates that "our yearning for connection is a primal human need"

(Goleman, 2006, p. 116). That is, nourishing relationships have a beneficial impact on our health and well-being, while toxic relationships act like slow poisons in our bodies (Albrecht, 2006). Therefore, students who feel connected to their teachers, to other students, and to the school itself are more motivated, do better academically, and are less likely to exhibit disruptive and violent behaviors (e.g., Hamre & Pianta, 2005; Klem & Connell, 2004; Libbey, 2004). Specifically, those who feel cared for and appreciated thrive, while, all too often, the students who don't feel connected with others exhibit inappropriate behavior and/or become socially withdrawn. Purkey and Novak (1984) summarized this principle when they wrote, "Humans need invitations the way flowers need sunshine. If students are to flourish in school they must have an environment that nurtures their potential" (p. 10). The "eight habits of the heart" for educators developed by Taulbert (2006) are presented in Table 2.2.

Table 2.2   The Eight Habits of the Heart

Nurturing Attitude

A nurturing attitude is characterized by unselfish caring and supportiveness and a willingness to share time.

Responsibility

Responsibility is showing and encouraging a personal commitment to each task.

Dependability

Dependability is being there for others through all the times of their lives—being a steady influence that makes tomorrow a welcome event.

Friendship

Friendship is the habit that binds people together when we take pleasure in each other's company, listen, laugh, and share good times and bad.

Brotherhood

Brotherhood is the habit that reaches beyond comfortable relationships to extend a welcome to those who may be different from ourselves.

High Expectations

High expectations involve believing that others can be successful, telling them so, and praising their accomplishments.

Courage

Courage is standing up and doing the right thing, speaking out on behalf of others, and making a commitment to excellence in the face of adversity or the absence of support.

Hope

Hope is believing in tomorrow—going beyond what we see because we have learned to see with our hearts.

SOURCE: Taken from Taulbert, C. L. (2006). *Eight habits of the heart for educators: Building strong school communities through timeless values.* Thousand Oaks, CA: Corwin.

Additional suggestions and strategies for developing positive relationships with students are described below:

- You communicate to others, including the students you teach, that you care by actively attending. For example, stopping what you are doing, orienting your body toward the other person, making eye contact, and listening and signaling that you're following what is said helps communicate to others that they are important to you.
- Express enthusiasm about the content you teach. Vary your facial expressions, use voice inflection, and alter the volume of your voice.
- Give attention to students when it is needed or set up a designated time to meet if the present circumstances do not permit it.
- Be professional in all verbal communication. Avoid swearing, sarcasm, or making any negative comments about any student's ethnicity, religion, disability, family, or sexual orientation.
- Caring is not the same as being a friend. It is in everyone's best interest that you not try to be students' friend. Maintain emotional distance so that you can make good decisions about how best to prepare them to meet current and future challenges.
- Being organized, prepared, and knowledgeable of the content you are going to teach will allow you to think clearly, to perform better, and to be more emotionally available for students.
- For young students, send a postcard or letter to new students before school begins letting them know that you look forward to working with them.
- Notice nonverbal indicators about how students are feeling and communicate those observations.
- Write positive comments on students' papers in addition to grades.
- Make an effort to understand the fads, fashions, popular heroes, latest films, sports teams, and television programs that presently motivate students. Use them as examples while teaching when appropriate.

- Organize group discussions for students to communicate about particular issues and feelings that affect them.
- Learn about students' personal interests and activities outside of school. To gather individual information from students, you can ask them to fill out a card or worksheet with some age-appropriate sentence starters. Following are examples of items to include:
  - The three things I like to do most are _____.
  - A television show I enjoy watching is _____.
  - My favorite foods are_____.
  - My favorite type of movie is _____.
  - My favorite type of music is _____.
  - My favorite sport is _____.
  - My favorite subject in school is _____.
  - When I graduate from high school I want to_____.
  - If I won a million dollars, I would _____.
- Find out which students are involved in clubs, teams, and band. Talk to students about their involvement and, when possible, attend the events to show your appreciation for their participation.
- Show students you have a sense of humor. Smile and casually joke with students throughout the day. You can also
  - laugh when you make mistakes.
  - share personal humorous stories and let students do the same.
  - read something humorous to the class on a regular basis.
  - put humorous items on worksheets and tests.
  - take pictures of students and let them develop humorous captions for the photos.
- Provide incentives for good performance rather than punishment for poor performance.
- When students miss a couple of days of school because of illness, call, text message, or e-mail to see how they are doing.
- Take a few minutes regularly to visit the student lunchroom. Sit and visit with different students each time.
- Provide opportunities for students to make choices, especially when they are of minor concern to you.
- Acquire and read aloud brief biographies of successful individuals who overcame hardships and challenges.
- Put motivational quotes or positive beliefs about the learning process on bulletin boards or on the whiteboard. Examples

include "It's okay to make mistakes. That's the way we learn," "We each learn in our own way," "It's smart to ask for help when you don't understand something," and "We can learn more when we are willing to risk."

- As noted above, the human brain is a social brain. Interaction, friendship, and companionship are intrinsically important to us. Opportunities for students to work together in pairs or small groups to review content, develop concept maps, take turns reading aloud, or complete an assignment or project are highly motivating and increase understanding of the content being studied.

Bottom Line

✓ Research indicates that students are more likely to succeed when they feel that adults in the school care about their learning, as well as about them as individuals. The findings apply across age, racial, ethnic, and income groups.

✓ Schools and teachers exert the second-greatest influence on how students perceive themselves and their abilities. Consequently, teachers' perceptions of students, as reflected in their behavior toward students, have the power to influence positively or negatively how students view themselves and how motivated they are to learn in school.

Build and Activate Background Knowledge

Learning is the treasure that will follow its owner everywhere.

—Chinese proverb

All students come to school with life experiences and concepts about the world. Each student's life experiences and concepts are stored and organized in memory structures called schema (*schemata* is the plural of *schema*). These schemata, or knowledge of the world, provide a foundation for understanding, learning, and remembering facts and ideas. Schemata enable us to organize large amounts of information into units of knowledge (Borich & Tombari, 1997). The more knowledge we acquire, the more elaborate our schemata become.

Classrooms are usually composed of students with varying amounts of background knowledge and schemata about the stories they are going to read or the content subjects they are expected to learn. In some cases, students don't have the background knowledge or the vocabulary they need to understand the topic of discussion or study. This lack of background knowledge, schemata, or vocabulary interferes with the learning process because when we learn, we incorporate new knowledge into old knowledge (Rose, Meyer, Strangman, & Rappolt, 2002). As a result, many of the students you teach will benefit from taking a little additional time to trigger or to fill in the gaps in their background knowledge. The following are suggestions for building and activating background knowledge:

- Have concrete experiences and hands-on exploration; visit places; attend live productions; or bring in physical objects, living creatures, or food related to the topic of study.
- Use visual aids, such as movies, CD-ROMs, Web sites with videos, photos, and graphics related to the subject matter to be learned or the story to be read.
- Preview the story you are going to read or content material you are going to learn about. Ask predicting questions to direct students' attention to the important aspects of the material. If you are using an expository text, such as a science, health, history, or geography book, first have the students look over the pages in the book. Then, use the pictures, graphics, boldface words, headings, and other organizational features to create prediction questions. For narrative texts, use the cover, the pictures, and some key words, such as names of the characters and the setting, to formulate prediction questions.
- Use the K-W-L strategy (Ogle, 1986), which consists of three general steps: (1) accessing what students know, (2) determining what they want to learn, and (3) recalling what they learned. Use a three-column format. For the first column, the **Know** section, guide students to identify what they know about the topic while you make the list in the column. For the second column, the **Want-to-Learn** section, students discuss and you list what they want to learn about the topic. For the third column, the **Learn** section, students discuss what they learned about the topic. The third column is completed at the end of the unit or after reading the material.
- Preteach essential vocabulary prior to the lesson or to reading the story. Teach the words that are critical to understanding the topic of study or the text you want students to read. Whenever

possible, it is best to avoid having students look up words in the dictionary or for you to provide dictionary definitions. Because dictionary definitions need to be concise due to space restrictions, they are often not helpful for students. Rather Beck, McKeown, and Kucan (2002) suggest that you provide students with descriptions using everyday language (e.g., "An *illusion* is something that looks like one thing but it is really something else or is not there at all."). After initially exposing students to the important vocabulary, you will want to use the words during lessons and structure brief blocks of time for students to review the words. See the section in Chapter 3 titled "Incorporate Activities" for ideas about ways to arrange opportunities for students to interact with vocabulary and key concepts.

- Bring in a variety of books conceptually related to the topic of study or to the theme of the story you are going to read. Try to select books that span a wide range of reading levels. Structure time for the students to examine the books or display them in an inviting manner and allow students to use them as they please.

- Use mental imagery. Guide students to think about the content or story by helping them imagine what they might experience. For example, if you were studying the Civil War, you could say, "Close your eyes and imagine that you are a soldier getting ready for the Battle of Gettysburg. What do you see? How do you feel?"

- Brainstorm information about the topic of study and create a web. You can start the web and have the students extend it. Transcribe the students' responses and try to generate links between the important concepts. See the section titled "Employ Graphic Organizers" in Chapter 3 for more specific information on this tool.

- Employ free recall. This strategy is similar to the above activity of brainstorming and creating a web, except no physical representation is developed. For example, prior to the beginning of a science unit, you could say, "We are going to be learning about tornadoes. What do you know about tornadoes?"

- Use peer tutoring for small groups of students who may benefit from additional exposure to the content concepts prior to the lesson, start of the unit, or reading of the story.

Bottom Line

✓ As a result of gaps in their experiential background, some students, such as those with disabilities, those who do not speak English as their first language, and those who are economically disadvantaged and who have not been exposed to the experiences that are supportive of school learning, may lack the schemata and/or vocabulary needed to follow abstract conversations, comprehend what is happening in a story, understand current events, or access information about the unit of study. Those students who do not bring the same language, conceptual, or experiential knowledge to their educational experience as their peers often demonstrate deficits that affect most aspects of the educational process. Consequently, it is important to incorporate techniques that clarify concepts and makes lessons relevant.

✓ Background knowledge is like Velcro: it helps new information stick. It builds connections between new and known information.

Increase Academic Learning Time

You will never find time for anything. If you want time you must make it.

—Charles Buxton (1823–1871), English Member of
Parliament, philanthropist, and author

Academic learning time (ALT) refers to the amount of time students are actively, successfully, and productively engaged in learning. ALT is highly correlated with academic achievement (Anderson & Walberg, 1993). Four factors contribute to ALT (Gettinger & Seibert, 2002):

1. *Allocated time*—The amount of time teachers plan to use for instructional activities

2. *Instructional time*—The proportion of allocated time that is actually spent on instructional activities

3. *Engagement rate*—The proportion of the instructional time during which students are actually engaged in learning (e.g., paying attention, completing assignments, interacting with peers about assigned work)

4. *Rate of academic success and productivity*—The proportion of engaged learning time during which students are performing meaningful and relevant instructional tasks with a relatively high rate of success

Although it is assumed that a major portion of the school day is spent on instructional activities, this is not always the case. Research (e.g., Hollowood, Salisbury, Rainforth, & Palombaro, 1995) indicates that as little as half of each school day may be devoted to instruction in some classrooms, depending on the teachers' managerial competencies, type of instruction used, grouping practices, and/or student characteristics. Specific sources of lost instructional time include the following:

- Student interruptions (e.g., disruptive behavior, leaving the room, peer conflicts)
- Teacher interruptions (e.g., disciplinary actions, distributing or collecting materials)
- Transitions (e.g., from subject to subject or room to room)
- Organizational activities (e.g., loudspeaker announcements, attendance, lunch counts, sharpening pencils)
- Undirected discussions (e.g., movies, sports, television programs)
- Visitors to the class (e.g., social interruptions from colleagues, collaboration with other service providers)
- Other disruptions (e.g., late start, fire drill, early dismissal)

Therefore, to be effective, you will want to schedule generous amounts of time for instruction and decrease the time spent in noninstructional activities. To make good use of instructional time, you will want to maintain a strong academic focus, which includes the following characteristics (Good & Brophy, 2007):

- Systematic, teacher-structured activities
- Lessons and content related to attaining specific goals
- Rapid pacing of lessons
- Ready availability of teaching materials
- High levels of student participation and responding
- Student accountability for homework
- Frequent monitoring of students' performance through quizzes and tests

To decrease the time spent in noninstructional activities, you will want to do the following:

- Facilitate efficient transitions by arranging the classroom's physical environment appropriately, establishing and enforcing rules, and using signals to indicate when activity shifts will occur.

- Establish and enforce procedures for students who finish work early and for those who need assistance.
- Teach and rehearse new lesson procedures (e.g., working in cooperative learning groups) or steps for using new equipment.
- Use your planning time to get ready for upcoming lessons (e.g., develop materials to hand out or to show by using technology rather than taking class time to write extensively on the board).
- Manage classroom discussions so they generate learning instead of allowing excessive off-task conversations to occur.
- Review directions for assigned tasks. To ensure that students understand instructions for activities, ask them to list the steps to be completed or paraphrase what they are expected to do.

Academic Learning Activities

Often students are provided with free time at the start of class, at the end of class, or when they say they have finished their independent practice work. Instead of letting students do nothing during these small blocks of time, use the time to review and to practice academic content. Examples of short practice activities you can adapt for your students include these:

- *Flash cards*—Have students create their own to practice another day with a peer.
- *Spelling*—Have students practice spelling key vocabulary words.
- Jeopardy-*type review*—You give facts; students need to develop questions.
- *Rapid-fire drill of facts*—Divide the class and keep score.
- *Developing questions*—Have students develop quiz questions about the unit of study to ask their peers another day.
- *Graphic organizer*—Give students a partially completed graphic organizer of content and have them finish it.
- *Notes*—Have students review their notes and identify and list key words to review with a peer another day.
- *Puzzles*—Develop puzzles, crosswords, and word searches related to the topic of study. (See Resources in the back of this book for Web sites that allow you to create these types of activities using content you specify.)
- *Summaries*—Write a summary of the lesson and share it with a peer.

Bottom Line

✓ The Organization for Economic Co-operation and Development (2007) reported that the United States ranks 36th of 40 industrialized nations in average weekly instructional time. U.S. students average 22.2 hours of instruction per week, as contrasted to 30.5 in Thailand (number 1) and 30.3 for Korea (number 2).

✓ Academic learning time (ALT) is a strong determinant of student academic achievement.

✓ You can increase ALT by preparing and delivering well-planned lessons, keeping students engaged in content-related learning activities, being organized, managing transition time, and using small blocks of time for practice and review.

Use Evidence-Based Practices

Facts don't cease to exist because they are ignored.

—Aldous Huxley (1894–1963),
English and American author

As consumers, the majority of us look for some form of verification, such as independent testing reviews, about the quality of products (e.g., tires, computers, cameras) we consider purchasing or services (e.g., restaurants, hotels) we would like to sample. Similarly, when one of our family members or friends becomes sick, evaluations of treatment options are often examined to determine the best choice. In each of these situations, we are looking for evidence of the quality or effectiveness of the product, service, or medical plan to guide our decision-making process.

Recently, the U.S. Department of Education began to require that education professionals apply the same type of scrutiny toward educational programs, products, practices, and policies that each of us uses on a daily basis as consumers. That is, specifically, the No Child Left Behind Act of 2001 requires professionals to consider the results of relevant scientifically based research, whenever such information is available, in making instructional decisions. NCLB defines *scientifically based research* as "research that involves the application of rigorous, systematic, and objective procedures to obtain reliable and valid knowledge relevant to education activities and programs" (Title IX, § 9101[37][A]). This guiding principle, which is also being implemented in the fields of medicine and psychology, is also referred to as evidence-based practice (EBP). The EBP orientation seeks to improve the quality of services provided to students by shifting to a culture in which judgments guided by data that can be inspected by a broad audience are valued over the opinions of individual experts (Carnine, 2000). More specifically, Chatterji (2008) suggests that the goals of the EBP perspective are useful for the following:

- *Schools*—To adopt educational programs, policies, and practices with defensible evidentiary support
- *Educators and educational policy makers*—To become informed consumers of research and evaluation evidence
- *Evidence users*—To begin to translate high-quality evidence into action, transforming themselves into effective, evidence-based practitioners

In addition to the legal mandates of NCLB for attending to EBPs, there are practical reasons why you should be guided by EBPs. First, it is a waste of money and time to use instructional procedures and/or materials that have not been demonstrated to be effective. Second, by using interventions that have a proven track record, you increase your probability of success. When students succeed, everyone—students, families, and you—feels better, and as a result, everybody is more motivated to work harder to accomplish achievement targets.

As you try to identify products and implement practices that have a body of research to support their use, how will you know which are effective and which are not? One challenge occurs when examining the professional journals and catalogs from businesses that develop and/or distribute educational products. All too often, they lead us to think that every product is effective with most populations. Of course, this is not the case. The truth of the matter is that many products and programs have been developed and marketed without being evaluated. Similarly, many practices and policies have been implemented prior to any type of research being conducted to determine if they actually produce the desired outcomes. Unfortunately, this gap between promise and verification exists in many aspects of our society.

The current demand for increased educational outcomes for students and the need for professionals to implement interventions that have a body of research to support their use requires you to increase your knowledge about the efficacy of the programs, products, practices, and policies you use. Consequently, when discussions occur with colleagues about issues such as reading and math curricula, schoolwide reform programs, afterschool programs, and new educational technologies, it is important to ask, "Where is the evidence?" to support the choice of one approach over another.

To help educators become more knowledgeable about EBPs, several agencies have been established to examine and summarize the quantity and quality of research to support the use of specific programs, products, practices, and policies. Below is a description of five agencies along with the URLs for accessing their Web sites and lists of the types of programs they have reviewed. Each agency continues to update its reviews.

1. The *What Works Clearinghouse* (WWC) (http://ies.ed.gov/ncee/wwc/) was established in 2002. The WWC identifies topics of interest to the education community (e.g., reading, math), gathers and reviews the research literature on the topics, determines the overall strength of the research base for each intervention, and publishes a report summarizing the strengths and limitations of the interventions. Examples of topics for which the WWC has produced reports include beginning reading, early childhood education, elementary school math, middle school math, character education, dropout prevention, and elementary English-language learners.

2. The *Promising Practices Network on Children, Families and Communities* (PPN) (www.promisingpractices.net) is operated by the RAND Corporation, a nonprofit institution that seeks to improve policy and decision making through research and analysis. Similar to the WWC, PPN examines the research on general topics as well as specific interventions, and it provides extensive reviews and summaries. Examples of topics for which the PPN has produced reports include behavior problems, reading, peer tutoring, life skills training, alcohol and drug prevention, and school readiness.

3. The *Best Evidence Encyclopedia* (BEE) (www.bestevidence.org) is a product of the Center for Data-Driven Reform in Education (CDDRE), a U.S. Department of Education-funded research center at Johns Hopkins University. The BEE provides brief readable "educator's summaries" of research similar to those provided by *Consumer Report,* as well as full-text reviews. Sample topics include elementary mathematics, reading for

English-language learners, secondary reading, technology in reading and math, and middle and high school math.

4. *The Campbell Collaboration* (C2) (www.campbellcollaboration.org) prepares and disseminates systematic reviews of research in education, crime, justice, and social welfare. Sample topics include volunteer tutoring programs and afterschool programs.

5. The *Evidence for Policy and Practice Information and Co-ordinating Centre* (EPPI-Centre) (www.eppi.ioe.ac.uk) is a United Kingdom-based association that provides a wide range of summaries of research. Sample topics include assessment, emotional and behavioral difficulties, cultural diversity, English teaching, inclusive education, learning and thinking skills, motivation, and science.

Bottom Line

✓ Evidence-based practice refers to an approach in which current, high-quality research evidence is integrated with professional expertise as well as student/family preferences and values into the process of making educational decisions (ASHA Joint Coordinating Committee on Evidence-Based Practice, 2005).

✓ Supporters of using evidence-based practices point to the improvements that have occurred in the fields of medicine (e.g., vaccines for polio, measles, and hepatitis; medications for hypertension), agriculture, and welfare policy. Embracing evidence as a basis for practice can be beneficial, as new and more effective practices progressively replace less effective practices.

Value Cultural and Linguistic Diversity

Variety's the very spice of life, that gives it all its flavor.

—William Cowper (1731–1800), English poet

Each year, the United States becomes more culturally and linguistically diverse. And all indications are that this trend will continue (U.S. Census Bureau, 2007a). As a result, it is very likely that the students in your classroom will reflect the increasing diversity that exists throughout the country.

Although many students who are culturally and linguistically diverse do well in school, a substantial number experience school failure and drop out (Gollnick & Chinn, 2006). The reasons these students fail to complete school are multifaceted and interconnected, but several factors are important to note. First, there is a shortage of culturally and linguistically diverse teachers. As a result, a lack of role models exists. Second, curriculum, textbooks, and instruction often do not include information about different cultural groups. Third, some teaching approaches (e.g., individual rather than cooperative efforts, public versus private performance) may not match the learning styles of students who are culturally and linguistically diverse. Fourth, a disproportionate number of students who are culturally and linguistically diverse are assigned to low-ability groups or placed in special education.

Teaching Students Who Are Culturally and Linguistically Diverse

Your attitude, behavior, and language related to diversity affect how welcome culturally and linguistically diverse students feel about being in school and set the tone for how the other students in the class think and feel about interacting with their classmates. Consequently, it is important for you take time to learn about your culture and how it influences your beliefs and actions. Simultaneously, reflect on your knowledge and beliefs about the cultural and linguistic diversity of the students you teach and use your reflections to create a personal mind-set, as well as a learning environment, that accepts and celebrates diversity. Questions, adapted from Montgomery (2001), to consider include these:

- What are my perceptions of students from different racial and ethnic groups?
- What are the sources of these perceptions?
- How do I respond to students based on these perceptions?
- What do I need to do to learn about the diverse backgrounds of the students I teach?
- What information, skills, and resources do I need to acquire to work effectively with students who are culturally and linguistically diverse?

A variety of strategies are presented here for you to consider so you can create learning environments that foster the academic and social success of students who are culturally and linguistically diverse:

- Learn as much as you can about the cultural and linguistic backgrounds of the students you teach. In addition to general background information, learn about issues such as family relationships and expectations, eye contact, personal space, gender roles, dialects, and conceptions of time.
- Have high expectations and believe that students are all capable of academic success irrespective of their cultural and linguistic background or socioeconomic status.
- Establish a learning community that is respectful of all its members, regardless of their clothes, customs, or languages, and respond decisively when intolerant behaviors occur.
- Make cultural diversity activities an ongoing part of the curriculum rather than a one-day acknowledgment of a cultural holiday.
- Accept invitations to have dinner with students and their families who are culturally and linguistically diverse. Doing so will help you gain insight into the influences on the students' attitudes and behaviors.
- Infuse multicultural literature, films, and art into the curriculum. Listen to music from different cultures. Learn games from other countries to play in physical education, at recess, or when students need a break to stretch and move around.
- Discuss the needs and wants universal to all humans, irrespective of culture, ethnicity, and language. Then compare the similarities and differences among cultures, including food, music, customs, languages, and holidays.
- Help students recognize and understand the tendency toward and the limitations of stereotypic thinking in real life and in the literature they read.
- Decorate the room, bulletin boards, and hallways with artwork and murals that reflect the cultures of the students you teach.
- Plan multicultural lunches in which students and their families work together to cook and serve cultural dishes.
- Develop a class calendar that recognizes the holidays and customs of many cultures.
- Acquire software that includes cross-cultural activities, as well as software that is available in several languages. Web sites for some businesses that produce such software are listed in Resources at the back of this book.

- Use trade books and films to supplement textbooks that present limited perspectives of historical or current events.

- Learn about second language acquisition, English as a second language (ESL) instructional approaches, and the challenges that students may experience in transitioning from interacting in their first language (L1)—basic interpersonal communication skills (BICS)—to learning in the second language (L2)—cognitive academic language proficiency (CALP).

- Teach students about the harmful effects of discrimination and how to treat others the way they would like to be treated.

- Invite successful professionals who are culturally and linguistically diverse to come to school to speak with students about their careers.

- Use cooperative learning, small workgroups, and peer tutoring so that students have opportunities to interact and exchange ideas with their fellow students.

Bottom Line

✓ The United States is one of the most culturally and linguistically diverse nations in the world. Researchers estimate that currently there are nearly 300 ethnic groups whose members can identify the national origins of their ancestors in the United States (Gollnick & Chinn, 2006).

✓ The demographics of the United States continue to change, causing a significant increase in the number of students who are culturally and linguistically diverse. To address the needs of these students, the structure of classrooms and the school environment needs to adapt so that all students have an equal opportunity to succeed in school.

✓ Most schools in the United States are based on mainstream Western culture. Children growing up in households with that cultural background often quickly adjust to the school environment, which includes behaviors such as obeying school rules, showing respect for authority, working independently, being punctual, cooperating with classmates, and delaying gratification. In contrast, some students from other cultural backgrounds find the inconsistencies between home and school difficult to resolve and experience school as a confusing and uncomfortable place.

> ✓ To meet the educational needs of all students, including those who come from culturally and linguistically diverse backgrounds, you want to help students increase their academic and social achievement by using teaching approaches and materials that are sensitive and relevant to students' cultural backgrounds and experiences, while simultaneously expecting and encouraging students to achieve at high levels.

Help English-Language Learners Succeed

A good education is like a savings account; the more you put into it, the richer you are.

—Anonymous

Students who are learning English as a second language are the fastest-growing segment of the school-age population in the United States. The National Clearinghouse for English Language Acquisition and Language Instruction Education Programs (NCLEA; 2006) reports that more than 10 percent of the student population (i.e., 5,074,572 students) is composed of limited English proficient students. Students who are English language learners in U.S. schools speak 350 different languages, with approximately 77% using Spanish as their native language. Vietnamese (2.4%), Hmong (1.8%) and Korean (1.2%) are the next most frequently spoken languages (NCELA, 2006).

Students who are English-language learners differ in more ways than only their native language. Some arrive at school being literate in their native language, with strong academic backgrounds and knowing some English. Others are not literate in their native language, have no experience with formal education, and have no knowledge of the English language. And, of course, many students who are English language learners have some background knowledge, are semiliterate in their native language, and know a little English.

Another difference among students who are English-language learners has to do with how well they succeed in school. While some individuals thrive in school, the majority of students who are English-language learners do not perform as well as their peers who enter school using English as their native language (U.S. Department of Education, 2007). For far too many students who are English-language learners, the ongoing lack of academic achievement and social affiliation leads to dropping out of school (Ruiz-de-Velasco & Fix, 2000).

The purpose of this section is to help you plan lessons and to establish social environments that promote learning and language development for students who are English-language learners. Three important points to consider when planning lessons for students who are English-language learners are the following:

1. Making the content comprehensible through the use of techniques such as visual aids, demonstrations, vocabulary previews, and student engagement (Echevarria, Vogt, & Short, 2004)

2. Structuring interaction among students (Saenz, Fuchs, & Fuchs, 2005)

3. Providing intensive, interactive English-language development instruction (Gersten et al., 2007)

The sections in this chapter titled "Build and Activate Background Knowledge" and—"Include Adaptations for Students With Special Needs"; in Chapter 3 titled "Differentiate Instruction" and "Employ Graphic Organizers"; and in Chapter 4 titled "Teach Study Skills" provide practical suggestions for helping you think about ways to make content accessible to students who are English-language learners. In addition, you will want to monitor the rate of your speech, the vocabulary you use, and the quality of directions you give. To reduce students' frustration and to increase their ability to complete their independent and collaborative work, get in the habit of providing instructions for assignments and activities in a step-by-step manner. Whenever possible, accompany the explanation with a visual representation, a demonstration, or a list of written procedures of what is expected.

Structuring opportunities for students to work together on practice activities and projects is beneficial for two reasons:

1. Students who collaborate tend to create scaffolding for one another's efforts and may develop more complicated ideas and strategies than students working independently (Ormrod, 2008).

2. Working with native English speakers creates opportunities to engage in conversations, as well as to practice using academic English (Echevarria, Vogt, & Short, 2004).

Cooperative learning, peer tutoring, and reciprocal teaching are three approaches that promote socialization and learning.

A strong relationship exists among vocabulary development, literacy, and academic achievement (Blachowicz & Fisher, 2000). As a result, consider undertaking some of the following suggestions when addressing the vocabulary and language development instruction for students who are English-language learners:

- Teach important words and concepts in advance of reading stories or content material. Only teach a handful of the most important words at one time.
- Provide explicit meanings of the important words and concepts related to the story or topic of study using "student-friendly definitions." For example, if you were reading a story about sailboats and one of the key words were *mast*, a "student-friendly definition" would be this: "You can tell if a ship is a sailboat if you see a mast. The mast holds up the big sail."
- Stimulate interest in words through activities such as word games, idioms, puns, figures of speech, and cartoons. The Resources at the back of this book includes several URLs for creating crossword puzzles and other similar activities.
- Immerse students in words by developing a "word wall," where key content vocabulary words are listed alphabetically, and using semantic webs, which show the nature of relationships between key words and a central concept.
- Provide instruction in root words, prefixes, and suffixes.
- Teach students how to conduct morpheme analysis (e.g., morpheme = *bi*, sample word = *bicycle*, approximate meaning = *two*).
- Many students who are English-language learners do not know many of the simpler words acquired through interaction by many native English speakers. Therefore, you will want to introduce and practice high-frequency words lists. Prioritize the list by the words that are used in conversation and appear often in literature.
- Avoid having students copy dictionary definitions. Due to the multiple meanings of words, this activity usually confuses students more than helps them. In addition, it is not very good use of academic learning time (ALT).
- Introduce and encourage students to use language for a variety of purposes. Examples of the different reasons we use language, suggested by Luckner (2002), are the following:
  o *Conversation*—An informal interaction between two or more people that generally involves an opening, an exchange of information, and a closing

- o *Description*—To convey an image or impression
- o *Direction*—To give instructions for completing a task
- o *Explanation*—To make factual information clear and understandable
- o *Narration*—To give an account of a real event or to tell a fictional story
- o *Persuasion*—To reach an agreement with others or to influence
- o *Questioning*—An expression of inquiry that invites or calls for a reply
- o *Writing*—The process of developing, selecting, combining, and arranging ideas into effective sentences, paragraphs, or longer units of information on paper or on other material or mediums (e.g., text messages, computers)

- Students benefit from repeated exposure to vocabulary. When students hear, see, write, and say words, they learn them better. Students who are read to often and/or who are engaged in reading a wide variety of texts learn more vocabulary. Consequently, it is important for you to know each student's interests and to suggest materials of interest that are at an appropriate level of difficulty for that student. Simultaneously, a variety of computer software and computer-assisted instructional vocabulary programs can be used to help provide the repeated exposures to words in different contexts that are necessary for successful word learning.

- Identify the students who are English-language learners who need additional instructional support by using assessments and progress-monitoring procedures. Because reading is critical for school success, early intensive reading instruction may help students learn the new language, as well as simultaneously learn to read in that new language. In addition to vocabulary, all dimensions of reading (i.e., phonemic awareness, phonics, fluency, and comprehension) should be assessed.

- Use resources such as texts written in the students' native language, native language Web sites, bilingual dictionaries, audiotapes, multimedia materials, and some of the Web sites listed in Resources at the back of this book.

Bottom Line

✓ The number of students whose first language is not English is increasing significantly. Whether to use students' native language or English as the language of instruction and/or for initial reading instruction has been the subject of great debate. Hopefully, additional research in the near future will provide more guidance. In the meantime, learn about and adhere to the policies of your school and district.

✓ Be conscious of using "wait time" appropriately so that students who are English-language learners have time to think about their answers and volunteer responses. Simultaneously, try not to fill in words for students when they are struggling to think of how to say something.

✓ Accepting and encouraging all students, regardless of their cultural heritage or their native language, and modifying instructional approaches so that all students can participate in the social and academic learning environment of your classroom is challenging, yet it is important for students' success. It will also provide you with well-deserved professional satisfaction.

Include Adaptations for Students With Special Needs

Education is not the filling of a pail, but the lighting of a fire.

—William Butler Yeats (1865–1939),
Irish poet and dramatist

According to The Center for Public Education (2008), approximately 13.6 percent of the students in grades K–12 have a disability. Most of those students receive all or most of their education in general education classrooms. In addition, the majority of these students receive accompanying special education and/or related services to help them succeed in school and after they leave school.

The purpose of this section is to provide some brief background information about a couple of laws that guide how students with disabilities should be provided educational services and to present a list of adaptations you can use to help students with special needs access lessons, demonstrate learning, and be active members of your classroom community. The adaptations are beneficial to use with students identified as having a disability, as well as with students who have delays in their learning as a result of family poverty, family instability, health problems, or limited English-language skills. You can acquire additional in-depth information about students with disabilities by accessing some of the resources listed in Resources and References and Suggested Readings at the back of this book.

Special Education Legislation

Individuals with Disabilities Education Act (IDEA)

Prior to 1975, many individuals with disabilities were denied access to public education. Some children and youth were forced to stay home or were placed in institutions; others were sent to private schools for which parents were required to pay. Many students who had mild or moderate learning problems dropped out of school long before graduating or acquiring marketable work skills. In 1975, Congress passed a law titled the Education for All Handicapped Children Act, now known as the Individuals with Disabilities Education Act (IDEA), which changed the face of public education in the United States. The law established the rights of students with disabilities to a free, appropriate public education. It also provided that this education would take place, to the maximum extent possible, in the least restrictive environment, which has come to be considered the general education classroom. In addition, the law specifically described the categories of disabilities that make students eligible to receive special education, the procedures for identifying a student as needing special education, and the rights of parents.

Another important component of the law is the Individualized Education Program (IEP). The IEP is developed annually by a team of professionals and includes a statement of the student's current level of functioning and a set of goals and short-term objectives for reaching those goals, as well as specifying who is responsible for delivering the student's services, how long the services will continue, where they will be provided, and how progress will be evaluated.

Section 504 of the Vocational Rehabilitation Act

Section 504 of the Vocational Rehabilitation Act is a civil rights law that prevents discrimination against all individuals with disabilities in programs that receive federal funds. Section 504 requires that buildings be physically accessible and that students have the right to a general education, extracurricular activities in their local schools, instructional and curriculum adaptations, and equal access to the services and programs available to students without disabilities. Through Section 504, some students who may not be eligible for services through special education (e.g., students with extreme allergies, heart conditions, AIDS, epilepsy, or social maladjustments) may be entitled to receive specific types of assistance to help them succeed in school. Section 504 does not require the development of an IEP; however, you are required to make adaptations to meet the learning needs of all students covered under Section 504. For students you teach who qualify for services under Section 504, it is best to work with a team of professionals to gather assessment data and to develop a written accommodations plan that includes information about the placement, available services, goals, accommodations, and who is responsible for the accommodations. The following section will detail some of the potential accommodations and modifications you can use with the students you teach.

Accommodations and Modifications

For many students with special needs or who demonstrate delays, you will need to use adaptations in instruction and assessment to help them succeed. Whenever possible, it is best to collaborate with a multidisciplinary team to help identify and implement ways to make the curriculum and social interactions accessible, as well as to ensure that the processes of assessment and grading are valid and reliable.

The term *adaptation* generally is used to explain changes that are made to help students learn best and to demonstrate what they are capable of doing. There are, however, some important distinctions in the types of adaptations about which you should be aware so that you can be certain that you and the other members of the multidisciplinary team are making decisions in the best interest of students.

- *Accommodation*—This type of adaptation focuses on how students access and demonstrate learning. Accommodations do not significantly change the instructional level, content, or performance criteria. The changes in process are made to provide a student equal access to learning and an equal opportunity to demonstrate what is known. Examples of accommodations are the use of a sign language interpreter, Braille, bilingual dictionaries, assistive technology, or books on tape.

• *Modification*—This type of adaptation substantially changes what students are expected to learn and demonstrate. Examples of modifications are allowing a student to read a text on the same topic as peers but at a much lower grade readability level, teaching a student how to use public transportation, and having a student answer test questions orally instead of having to write responses. Modifications change the course objectives, assessment content, grading process. and possibly the type of diploma that will be received.

The decision to use accommodations or modifications should be discussed and agreed upon by all members of the multidisciplinary team. The choice of which specific adaptations to use will depend on the goals for the students, the needs of the students, and your instructional style. In general, you will want to choose adaptations based on three guidelines:

1. Those that are most likely to affect the student positively

2. Those that require the least time and effort on your part

3. Those with which you feel comfortable

Table 2.3 is a list of potential adaptations, which have been adapted from Luckner and Denzin (1998). The list is divided into seven general areas. Keep in mind that you cannot be certain that a specific adaptation will be effective for a particular student or, in fact, that it will not actually impede the student's learning. Therefore, you should always evaluate the adaptations you use with students soon after implementation to make sure they are effective. Again, whenever possible, involve members of the multidisciplinary team in selecting and evaluating the effectiveness of the accommodations and modifications used with students.

Table 2.3   Sample Adaptations

Environmental

- Seat student in best place to permit attending and participation.
- Use a semicircular seating arrangement.
- Reduce noise and reverberation with carpeting, draperies, acoustic ceiling tile, and acoustical wall treatments.
- Keep desks away from distractions, such as open doorways and pencil sharpeners.
- Arrange for a quiet place for students to use when becoming upset.
- Post schedules for students to follow.

Behavioral

- Provide consistent expectations and consequences with regard to classroom routines and rules.
- Place general rules and behavior expectations on charts displayed in the room or on a sheet of paper placed on the student's desk.
- Use interest inventories to identify positive and negative reinforcers for each individual.
- Use assignment books and/or folders to increase organizational and memory skills.
- Provide regular feedback and check progress often.
- Develop a home-school contract with student's family whereby when specific behaviors are demonstrated in school, the student receives a specified reinforcer at home.
- Send a daily or weekly report card home.
- Use corrective feedback (e.g., "I would like you to take out a book and read when you finish your work, rather than bothering the person sitting next to you.")
- Increase frequency of descriptive praise (e.g., "You really paid attention and stayed in your seat for the past 15 minutes.")
- Use a behavioral contract, which is a written agreement between teacher and student regarding student behavior and agreed-upon consequences.
- Use response cost procedures (e.g., taking away a privilege, points, or a reward).
- Use time-outs.
- Limit the number of distractions by establishing an isolated work/study area.
- Teach the student anger control strategies.

Input: Teaching Content

- Preteach and review important vocabulary and concepts.
- Modify class schedule to reduce fatigue (e.g., include opportunities for active involvement).

- Provide a study guide of the key concepts, questions, vocabulary, and facts when introducing new material. Include page numbers where information can be found in the textbook.
- Provide the student with a copy of your notes.
- Highlight key words or concepts in printed material.
- Supplement the lesson with visual materials (e.g., real objects, pictures, photographs, charts, videos).
- Provide manipulatives for multisensory, hands-on instruction or activities.
- Use peer tutoring.
- Use cooperative learning experiences.
- Use games for drill and practice.
- Use concise statements or simplified vocabulary.
- Use a "buddy system" whereby one student helps another student stay on-task.
- Write short summaries of the lesson or of the chapters of the textbook.
- Use a peer tutor, paraprofessional, or volunteer to review work, important concepts, vocabulary, and facts with the student.
- Use commercial software to provide practice and review material.
- Divide and organize lengthy directions into multiple steps.
- Demonstrate directions to clarify what needs to be undertaken.
- Check for understanding by having students restate the directions.
- Break long-range projects into short-term assignments.
- Post the date on the board when assignments and projects are due. Remind students frequently.
- Increase the number of practice examples of a rule, concept, or strategy prior to assigning seatwork or homework.
- Shorten the length of assignments and provide additional opportunities for practice.
- Teach organizational skills and assist the student in generalizing these skills.
- Provide duplicate sets of materials for family use and review.
- Have students summarize at the end of the lesson.

Output: Students Practicing and Demonstrating What They Have Learned

- Allow more time to complete assignments.
- Allow students to make models, role-play, develop skits, and create art projects to demonstrate their understanding of the information.
- Allow written or drawn responses to serve as alternatives to oral presentations.
- Allow the student to use a computer/word processor.
- Use cooperative learning experiences to develop cooperative small-group projects.
- Use a peer tutor, paraprofessional, or volunteer to work with the student on a task.

(Continued)

(Continued)

Social

- Make books about exceptionalities and diverse cultures available.
- Invite adults with exceptionalities or from diverse cultures to come to school and share stories.
- Implement a "circle of friends" program.
- Structure activities and experiences so that students of differing ability levels work together.
- Teach units on social topics (e.g., friendship, avoiding fights, emotions, stealing, dating, dealing with divorce).
- Provide direct instruction on specific social skills (e.g., starting conversations, giving compliments, responding to criticism).
- Encourage students to become involved in extracurricular activities.

Evaluation

- Use a peer tutor, paraprofessional, or volunteer to work with the student to review for test.
- Allow tests to be taken with the special education teacher or paraprofessional.
- Provide extra time to complete tests and quizzes.
- Allow test items to be read to the student.
- Modify vocabulary used in test items to match the student's abilities.
- Modify the number of test items.
- Provide shorter tests on a more frequent basis.
- Chart progress or lack of progress.
- Provide additional information to explain test questions and instructions.
- Allow the student to use notes, a study guide, or the textbook when taking tests.
- Evaluate daily work and participation in addition to tests.
- Use projects or portfolios in lieu of tests.
- Provide graphic cues (e.g., arrows, stop signs) on answer forms.
- Give alternative forms of the test (e.g., matching, multiple-choice, fill-in-the-blank, true/false, short-answer, or essay questions).
- Allow student to respond orally or in sign language and have a scribe fill in bubbles in the test book or write the student's responses to the test items.
- Use assistive technology to communicate responses to the test items.

Grading

- Use the IEP as the criteria for grading.
- Develop a contract as the basis for grading.
- Use a pass/fail system.
- Write descriptive comments and give examples regarding student performance.
- Use a checklist of competencies associated with the course and evaluate according to mastery of the competencies.

Bottom Line

✓ Students with disabilities, students with delays, gifted and talented students, and students from ethnically and culturally different backgrounds are all part of the makeup of the current student population. This diversity provides opportunities for you and the students you teach to learn from each other, to develop a deeper understanding and respect for people's similarities and differences, and to use these similarities and differences to develop effective classrooms and supportive school environments.

✓ The types of adaptations you decide to use should be based on the students you teach, the learning environment, and the curriculum goals. You can individualize the curriculum goals by adding or reducing the material and skills to be learned, varying the levels of difficulty of the content, and having students demonstrate their knowledge and skills in different ways.

3

Teaching Effectively Part II

Teaching to the Whole Student

Enhance Social Relationships and Promote Learning

Alone we can do so little; together we can do so much.

—Helen Keller

Social relationships play an important role in our lives during school and at work. Social relationships are essential because they add quality to our lives, expose us to a variety of role models and standards for appropriate ways of behaving, and increase motivation for attending school and holding jobs (Snell & Janney, 2000). Research studies (e.g., Carnevale, Gainer, & Meltzer, 1988; Dowd & Liedtka, 1994; Secretary's Commission on Achieving Necessary Skills, 1991) indicate that employers consider the general competencies of initiative, self-confidence, and collaboration to be most important for success and fulfillment in the world of work. Goleman (1998) used those general areas, as well as his own research, to develop a program that focuses on five areas:

1. Self-awareness
2. Self-regulation
3. Motivation
4. Social awareness
5. Social skills

He, along with other researchers (e.g., Elias & Arnold, 2006), contends that students need instruction as well as opportunities to learn how to form relationships, to communicate effectively, to be sensitive to others' needs, and to get along with others to succeed in the different environments they will live in once they leave school—work, home, and community.

In addition to developing social interaction skills, interactive learning is beneficial for students because it causes them to make their thought processes visible to their peers, which causes their knowledge about the topic at hand to be examined, built upon, strengthened, and, if necessary, reshaped (Resnick, 1987). Given the importance of increasing students' ability to interact with each other in appropriate ways, as well as for you to have a variety of teaching methods to promote academic learning, two effective approaches—cooperative learning and peer tutoring—are presented here.

Cooperative Learning

Cooperative learning is a method of instruction in which students are organized into small groups to complete assignments or projects. Numerous research studies over the past 20 years (e.g., Nastasi & Clements, 1991; Rohrbeck, Ginsburg-Block, Fantuzzo, & Miller, 2003) have demonstrated that when cooperative learning activities are designed and structured appropriately, academic achievement levels are equal to or greater than individualistic or competitive teaching methods. Simultaneously, students gain opportunities to develop and practice their social skills and problem-solving abilities, which in our current collaborative, technological economy are critical skills for succeeding in the world of work.

While cooperative learning can be beneficial for students, simply placing them in groups to work together can have some negative effects as well. For example, some students may not have the necessary social skills, such as requesting clarification, asking a peer for help, negotiating, or integrating divergent viewpoints, to work cooperatively. Other students may overemphasize the social aspect (e.g., talking with friends, showing off, clowning around) rather than positively contributing to the task at hand. Also, dominant students may monopolize groups, which may cause passive students to become detached. Consequently, you will want to implement many of the specific strategies discussed below to promote effective cooperative learning experiences.

Several models of cooperative learning (e.g., Johnson & Johnson, 1999; Putnam, 1998; Slavin, 1995) exist. However, four common elements are found across the various models:

1. Students in the groups have positive interdependence; that is, the group works together to achieve their goal.

2. Students work together, face-to-face, to complete the work.

3. Students have individual accountability.

4. Social skills, such as active listening and praising peers, are emphasized.

Cooperative learning can be used to teach most subjects, using a variety of learning tasks and engaging all age groups. It serves as an excellent alternative to group lessons or individual seatwork. If you are not familiar with cooperative learning, it is best to start small, implementing it with one subject until the process feels comfortable for you. Then begin to use it with different subjects and make adaptations based on your preferences, as well as the needs and abilities of the students.

Implementing cooperative learning initially requires a little more planning time. Attending to the following four phases and subcomponents (adapted from Johnson, Johnson, & Holubec, 1993) will help the process go smoothly:

Phase 1—Planning:

- Specify instructional objectives.
- Decide on the size of the groups.
- Assign students to the groups.
- Arrange the room to accommodate working groups.
- Arrange instructional materials.

Phase 2—Preparing students:

- Assign roles to ensure interdependence.
- Explain the academic task.

- Structure individual accountability.
- Specify desired social skills behaviors.

Phase 3—Monitor and intervene:

- Monitor students' behavior.
- Provide task assistance when necessary.
- Intervene to teach collaborative skills.

Phase 4—Evaluation and processing:

- Provide closure to the lesson.
- Evaluate the quality and quantity of students' learning.
- Assess how well the groups functioned.

Peer Tutoring

Peer tutoring involves pairs of students working together to practice or learn a new skill. One student assumes the role of the tutor, helping the other student, the tutee, to increase his or her learning of specific content (e.g., science unit definitions) or to improve skills (e.g., reading fluency). Research (e.g., Greenwood, Carta, & Hall, 1988) suggests that peer tutoring in some instances leads to greater academic gains than traditional types of instruction. It also benefits both the tutor and the tutee (Fuchs, Fuchs, Mathes, & Simmons, 1997). The tutee receives the advantage of additional one-on-one instruction, while the tutor is required to study the material in greater depth, given the expectation of teaching it to another student. Finally, peer tutoring has been demonstrated to foster a positive attitude toward school for both the tutor and the tutee (Heron, Welsch, & Goddard, 2003).

Classwide peer tutoring has been used with a variety of subjects and a wide range of students. Consider using the following steps, adapted from Friend and Bursuck (2002), when using a classwide peer tutoring program:

1. Assign students to tutoring pairs or randomly divide the class into two groups and set up pairs within both groups.

2. Assign each pair to one of two classroom teams.

3. Teach all students a specific series of steps for presenting and practicing content.

4. Teach all students specific strategies for correcting tutees when a wrong response is given and for rewarding correct responses.

5. Provide pairs with daily assignments.

6. Teach tutors to keep score. When a tutee answers correctly, a point is awarded to that team.

7. Count points, post scores, and announce the winning team.

8. Reward the winning team with an acknowledgement or a privilege.

9. Reverse the tutor/tutee roles each session or have both stdents take the tutor role within each session.

Another option is the cross-age tutoring approach, which occurs by pairing older students to serve as tutors for younger students. The tutoring sessions provide the younger students with increased opportunities to practice designated skills, as well as chances to interact with an older, more mature student on a regular basis. This approach can be used with entire classes (e.g., fifth-grade students in one class work with a class of first-grade students on sight words every Tuesday at 10:45 AM, or seniors in high school are paired with freshmen to review chemistry vocabulary and concepts) or with individual arrangements.

Bottom Line

✓ Social interactions, interpersonal relations, and communication with others influence academic learning.

✓ Cooperative learning and peer-tutoring approaches can have very positive effects on students' academic and social skills. However, they must be carefully planned and systematically implemented.

Ask Good Questions

Good teaching is more a giving of right questions than a giving of right answers.

—Josef Albers (1888–1976),
German and American artist and educator

Why Should You Care About the Questions You Ask?

You will want to use questions effectively for six reasons:

1. Questions allow you to monitor students' understanding of the content being presented. If you find out through questioning

that students have not understood the material, you can adjust your instruction. Those adjustments could include the use of more examples and nonexamples, explanations of important vocabulary, and/or slowing down the rate of presentation.

2. The process of responding to questions allows students to practice actively using the content being taught.

3. Questions can be used to foster discussions about the content. These discussions can be conducted as a class, in small groups, or in pairs.

4. Asking questions can help maintain students' attention. Dividing lessons into shorter sections that include opportunities for review and practice can help students stay focused and prevent potential behavior problems.

5. Questions can be used to stimulate interest and activate background knowledge about the upcoming topic of study (e.g., "What do you know about earthquakes?").

6. Questions can be used to encourage higher-level thinking. Higher-level questions encourage students to go beyond the information itself and to construct more sophisticated understandings.

What Types of Questions Are There?

Questions are often described as being either lower-level or higher-level questions. Both types of questions are important. Lower-level questions are usually convergent questions. They involve repetition and review of previously covered information. They are often used in the early stages of learning, in learning basic skills and facts, or in building fluency. In general, when using lower-level questions, you will want to ask questions that require simple, direct answers (e.g., "What is the formula for finding the area of a rectangle?"), and you will want to maintain a fast pace (e.g., "Right, Teshon, now who can tell me the formula for finding the perimeter of a rectangle?"). Higher-level questions require more in-depth thinking and more elaborate responses (e.g., "What is your evaluation of the effect of technology on daily living?"). Consequently, higher-level questioning should proceed at a slower pace than lower-level questioning.

How Can I Ask Good Questions?

A helpful tool for developing questions is a hierarchal model of cognitive processes created by Anderson et al. (2001), who modified Bloom's taxonomy (Bloom & Krathwohl, 1977). The revised taxonomy is composed of six cognitive processes that progress from simple to more complex. Listed below are the six cognitive processes, presented in order from less to more complex; short descriptions of each process; and sample question stems you can use to develop questions to promote students' thinking.

Cognitive Processes

1. *Remember*—Recognize or recall information previously learned.

   Question stems—Tell, describe, how many, label, define, name, when, where, list, identify

2. *Understand*—Construct meaning from instructional materials.

   Question stems—Explain, estimate, give examples, illustrate, differentiate, interpret, summarize

3. *Apply*—Use previously learned information in a new and unfamiliar situation.

   Question stems—Demonstrate, examine, compute, predict, produce, provide, assess

4. *Analyze*—Break information into its constituent parts and try to identify the interrelationships among the parts.

   Question stems—Compare, classify, contrast, distinguish, prioritize, separate, analyze

5. *Evaluate*—Make judgments about information using certain criteria or standards.

   Question stems—Assess, criticize, defend, evaluate, judge, justify, rate, select

6. *Create*—Put knowledge and/or procedures together to form a pattern not clearly there before.

   Question stems—Design, develop, formulate, generate, organize, produce, propose, perform

What Are Some Guidelines for Using Questions?

- Provide a balance between lower-level and higher-level questions.
- Prepare questions in advance so you can be sure to ask lower-level or higher-level questions and so that you are able to follow up on students' responses spontaneously, rather than trying to figure out what your next question is going to be.
- Use wait time; that is, wait three to five seconds before selecting a student to respond to a question and wait again before responding to the student's reply. Research (e.g., Tobin, 1987) suggests that when teachers wait at least three seconds, there is increased student participation and better quality student responses and students show higher achievement.
- Phrase questions clearly. Vague questions, such as "What about Central America?" cause students to spend time trying to understand what you are asking rather than thinking about an appropriate response.
- Ask one question at a time. If you ask a couple of questions simultaneously, students can get confused.
- Establish and enforce a routine for responding to questions. Teach and remind students about the routine you want to use when having class discussions. To avoid shouting, consider having students raise their hands and be recognized before they speak.
- State the question first and then call on a specific student to respond. If you call out a student's name prior to asking the question, other students may disengage because they think that only the student called on needs to reply.
- Use question prompts when students struggle with lower-level questions. When you ask a question and a student doesn't know the answer, rather than simply repeating the question or skipping to another student, try to help the student maintain his or her dignity by making the question a little easier. You can do this by (1) turning it into a true/false or yes/no question, (2) turning it into a multiple-choice question, or (3) modeling the response with related content (e.g., "The capital of Colorado is Denver, so what is the capital of Wyoming?").
- Attempt to keep all students engaged by calling on nonvolunteers as well as volunteers.
- Encourage students to defend their responses. Ask follow-up questions, such as "Why do you think that?" and "How do you know?"

- Occasionally, have all students write down an answer to a question or turn to their neighbors with the answer before calling on students to respond orally to the entire class.

Bottom Line

✓ Teachers ask hundreds of questions in the course of a day. Questions serve many purposes, including review and practice, stimulating students' curiosity about an upcoming lesson, keeping students on-task, and fostering higher-level thinking so students can apply what they have learned to new situations. Given the critical role of using questioning strategies for being an effective teacher, it is important for you to become skilled at developing and asking good questions.

✓ Fact-based questions are useful for helping students acquire and review basic knowledge and skills. Higher-level questions, which call for inferences, applications, justifications, and solutions to problems, are also very important to integrate into lessons because they require students to apply and generalize the content they are learning.

Integrate Technology

The Internet is becoming the town square for the global village of tomorrow.

—Bill Gates, software developer,
cofounder of Microsoft and philanthropist

In our current global, digital world, technology is rapidly changing how people learn, work, and live. Technology is a valuable tool and has great potential for helping you deliver quality instruction, particularly when combined with other key factors, such as those discussed in Chapter 2 in the sections titled "Attend to the Science of Teaching" and "Apply the Art of Teaching."

You will want to use technology for four specific purposes:

1. *To enrich and extend the curriculum.* Technology opens doors to experiences that students can't access in other ways, and these

experiences can expand both the depth and breadth of the curriculum.

2. *To reinforce skills that you have previously introduced.* Technology can present guided practice activities, monitor students' responses, and provide students with immediate feedback.

3. *To adapt learning activities to meet the needs of specific students.* Some students will require adaptations to the curriculum because they have a disability, have limited English skills, or learn content very rapidly. Technology provides an avenue for you to individualize instruction to meet their unique needs.

4. *To save yourself time and effort.*

In addition, research (e.g., CEO Forum on Education and Technology, 2001; Cradler, McNabb, Freeman, & Burchett, 2002; Heafner, 2004) has documented that the effective use of technology increases students'

- motivation;
- time on-task;
- amount of work completed;
- critical thinking, research, and organizational skills;
- self-confidence; and
- interest in content.

The two most consistently identified barriers to the effective integration of technology into teaching and learning are time and a lack of technical and professional support (Dickward, 2003). However, for students to be prepared for the world of work, for citizenship, and for lifelong learning, they will need to develop technology-related competencies (Panel on Education Technology, 1997). Because the use of technology by students is greatly influenced by the ability of their teachers to integrate technology into their teaching (Todd & McNergney, 1999), you will want to constantly upgrade your technology knowledge and skills. Please see the section titled "Be a Lifelong Learner" in Chapter 6 for examples of training that can help you become comfortable with using technology effectively in the classroom.

Learning Technologies

A variety of learning technologies are available for you to use and to teach students to use. Following are frequently used computer-based technologies and examples of their practical application.

Word Processing

Word processing software is a computer application, used to produce any sort of printable material, that permits editing, saving, and retrieving of documents. Word processors are the most popular tool used in schools. They allow users to write, edit, revise, format, and print text. Following are some examples:

- Class or school newsletters
- Calendar of class events
- Assignments and test dates
- Graphic organizers
- Development and storage of documents, such as practice activities, quizzes, tests, notices of upcoming events, and permission slips, for future use
- Answer keys for quizzes and tests
- Educational goals and objectives
- Lesson plans
- Graphs
- List of classroom rules
- Lecture notes
- Labels and tags
- Address lists
- Certificates and coupons

Spreadsheets

Spreadsheet software is a computer application that provides a grid arranged in rows and columns with which you can manipulate data in the form of an electronic worksheet. You can use spreadsheets to keep track of data and to calculate descriptive statistics. You can also teach students to compare multiple variables, such as the amount of precipitation across the states in a region, population of countries, cost of living in different cities, types of governments, and annual salaries of a variety of careers. Following are some examples:

- Recording and tracking students' grades
- Organizing any data
- Plotting expenses
- Making visual representations of numbers or events

E-mail

Short for "electronic mail," *e-mail* is a method of composing, sending, storing, and receiving messages over electronic communication systems. Following are some examples:

- Contacting colleagues, families and students
- Establishing pen pals with students from other schools, states, or countries
- Posting and reading messages on listservs
- Posting and reading messages on discussion boards, which allow students to post comments and read responses about a posed question, specific reading material, or particular issues.

World Wide Web

The World Wide Web is a system of interlinked, hypertext documents accessed via the Internet. Following are some examples:

- Web pages
- Pictures of class activities
- News on current events
- Digital portfolios
- Links related to unit of study
- Practice activities
- Instructional materials (e.g., information, photos, videos, simulations, games)
- Online databases (e.g., the U.S. Census Bureau and the national Climatic Data Center)
- Discussion groups
- Music
- Virtual tours (e.g., of countries, cities, museums, exhibits, government agencies, historical documents)
- Professional development
- Government reports
- Textbook publishers
- Video chats
- WebQuests, an inquiry-based activity in which some or all of the information comes from resources on the Internet. The six elements of a WebQuest suggested by Norton and Sprague (2001) are as follows:

  1. *Introduction*—Sets the stage and provides some background information.

2. *Task*—This is what needs to be completed and the due date.
3. *Process for completing the task*—Consists of clearly described steps.
4. *Marked Web sites for completing the task*—These are the documents and databases students should examine.
5. *Organization expectations*—These include how time should be used and how learning will be demonstrated.
6. *Evaluation*—There is an examination of the completed project.

  o WebQuests should be tied to the state standards and connected to the curriculum. Types of WebQuests noted by Thorsen (2003) include the following:

- *Contemporary problems*—Examples include population, energy, and poverty.
- *Use of imagination*—Examples include journeys to distant places, such as Mars, or inaccessible places, such as the inner ear.
- *Common life activities*—Examples include applying for a job or visiting a city.
- *Evaluating history*—Examples include important inventions and discoveries, as well as elections, wars, and laws.

Computer Graphics

With computer graphics, one can integrate images into the teaching and learning process. Following are some examples:

- Printing graphics to create banners, certificates, or signs
- Drawing programs
- Painting programs
- Idea processors to develop graphic organizers and webs
- Animation programs
- Clip art
- Web-based graphics and pictures
- Scanners
- Digital cameras

Presentation Software

Presentation software is a computer application that allows users to display information in a variety of formats (e.g., text, video, audio, graphic, and animation). Examples of presentation software include PowerPoint and HyperStudio. One of the primary benefits of using presentation software is that due to the integration of multiple for-mats, it accommodates a variety of learning styles. In addition, when students develop presentations using such software, they are required to organize and synthesize the content. Following are some examples of how presentation software can be used:

- Pictures
- Animation
- Short movies
- Graphic organizers
- Electronic portfolios

Educational Software

Educational software is a collection of computer programs, pro-cedures, and documentation that perform specific tasks on a com-puter. Benefits include opportunities for individualization and the ability to match technological applications with the curriculum; also, students often find some of the features motivating. Following are some examples:

- Subject matter (e.g., language arts, math, science, social studies, art, music) software
- Tutorials
- Drill-and-practice
- Simulations and modeling
- Discovery
- Games

Assistive Technology

This category of technology includes assistive, adaptive, and rehabilitative devices used to promote independence for people with disabilities by enabling them to perform tasks by providing enhance-ments to or changed methods of interacting with the technology needed to accomplish such tasks. Following are some examples:

- Touch screens
- Expanded keyboards
- Screen readers (i.e., text-to-speech synthesizers)
- Speech recognition devices
- Communication boards
- Captioned films
- Braille translation software

Bottom Line

✓ Technology will be a central part of the future for the students you teach. What shape the technology will take and how it will change their lives is impossible to predict. However, you can be certain that technology will play an integral role in everyone's life. Consequently, technology needs to be integrated into classrooms so that students are ready and motivated to live and work in the technology-based global economy.

✓ Numerous education resource sites on the Internet can give you access to fellow teachers, blogs, lesson plans, materials, and opportunities for professional development. See Resources in the back of this book for URLs (Web site addresses) to browse.

Differentiate Instruction

Don't find fault; find a remedy.

—Henry Ford (1863–1947), industrial innovator and founder of Ford Motor Company

Classrooms are true mosaics of America. Most classes are composed of a mixture of students with different levels of ability; ethnic, cultural, and/or linguistic backgrounds; experiences; family situations; levels of maturity; and interests. For these diverse groups of individuals to succeed in school, you will want to plan and deliver instruction that is tailored to the unique strengths, preferences, and challenges of the students you teach. You can do this by adding to or reducing the material and skills to be learned and/or by having students demonstrate their knowledge and skills in different ways (Tomlinson, 2005).

Differentiated instruction allows you to teach all students the same content but to vary the level of difficulty based on the students in your class. To ease the planning process, you may want to think about preparing lessons for the following four groups of students:

1. Students who have strong background knowledge of the content or process and/or who learn quickly

2. Students who benefit from grade-level instruction

3. Students who need some additional preteaching, review, and practice

4. Students who need a specialized program and support in addition to participating in the general education curriculum

Step 1: Identify Concepts and Goals

To differentiate instruction, you will want to begin by identifying the concepts and skills you want to teach. These will be based upon your curricular goals, which should be aligned with your state and district standards. Once you have determined the unit of study you are going to teach, you will want to begin the planning process by sequentially deciding the following:

1. What content and skills will *all* students learn? What subject matter, activities, and products will *all* students study, do, and produce?

2. What content and skills will *most* students learn? In addition to what *all* students will learn, what supplementary facts, concepts, activities, and/or products will *most* students study, do, and produce?

3. What content and skills will *some* students learn? In addition to what *all* students and *most* students will learn, what additional information, assignments, or products will a few students access, complete, and/or create that will enable them to enhance their understanding of the topic of study?

Step 2: Determine Teaching Methods

The second step will be to determine what teaching methods you will use to help students learn the content and develop skills. If you plan to use lectures and discussions, you can supplement the lessons by using graphic organizers, pictures, or other forms of technology. To help the students you anticipate may need additional exposure to the content, you can do the following:

- Have the text read and captured on CD and let students listen to it.
- Provide a copy of your notes.
- Have a paraprofessional or volunteer preteach and review important concepts and vocabulary.
- Use peer tutoring.
- Develop review cards that can be used for practice and provide time for students to use the cards by playing games such as Concentration, Jeopardy, or Taboo.

For students whom you anticipate will have extensive background knowledge of the topic or who are able to access content material quickly, you can use the following strategies:

- Create an independent or small-group activity related to the topic of study (see the subsection in Chapter 2 "Attend to the Science of Teaching: Promoting Higher-Level Thinking Skills: Active Learning" for a discussion of learning contracts).
- Allow individuals or small groups of students to conduct a WebQuest (see the "Integrate Technology" section above).
- Allow students to access primary source documents related to the topic of study from document collections such as the National Archives and the Library of Congress.
- Have students create a graphic comic of the content to share with their peers.
- Ask students to critique or analyze information using a set of standards or from another person's or a group's perspective (e.g., the impact of the Americans with Disabilities Act from the viewpoint of an individual who uses a wheelchair as compared to an owner of a small business).

If you plan to have students read the material in a textbook prior to having a group discussion or prior to completing independent seatwork, you may want to use one or more of the following strategies:

- Use materials that present similar content but at a lower or at a higher readability level.
- Directly teach important vocabulary and concepts prior to asking students to read the material.
- Develop and distribute study guides that emphasize the important information in the text.
- Have a student who reads well, a paraprofessional, or a volunteer read the material to students who don't read fluently.
- Allow students to preview the headings and the pictures before reading the text.
- Highlight the material that is critical for students to know.
- Provide a list of questions to be discussed before reading the text and allow students to look for the answers.
- Provide students with an outline of the main ideas and a glossary of vocabulary words prior to reading.

Step 3: Assign In-Class Work and Homework

The third step is to determine what in-class and homework assignments you will have students complete. Options to consider are the following:

- Work in small groups on in-class assignments.
- Reduce or increase the difficulty level of the assignment based on the individual student.
- Shorten the length of assignments.
- Provide extra time to complete assignments.
- Eliminate copying from the board.
- Allow students to respond orally or to dictate their responses to a peer, paraprofessional, or volunteer.
- Use computers for review and practice.
- Establish learning centers with differentiated level tasks.
- Provide extra review, drill, and practice.

Step 4: Evaluate Student Learning

The final step is to determine how you are going to evaluate student learning. Following are some alternatives:

- Let students dictate their responses to test items.
- Record the test and allow students to record their answers.
- Conduct short, frequent quizzes with feedback rather than an end-of-unit test.
- Allow students to make models, role-play, develop skits, produce a video, or create art projects to demonstrate their understanding of the information.
- Allow written or drawn responses to serve as alternatives to oral presentations.
- Allow students to use a computer/word processor.
- Permit students to have open-book tests.
- Permit students to conduct independent investigations related to the topic of study.
- Provide extra time to complete tests and quizzes.
- Modify vocabulary used in test items to match student abilities.
- Have students develop multimedia presentations (e.g., PowerPoint).
- Give alternative forms of the test (e.g., matching, multiple-choice, fill-in-the-blank, true-false, short-answer, or essay questions).

Bottom Line

✓ Students differ across a wide variety of factors, including readiness, experiences, gender, family composition, ethnicity, culture, home language, intelligences, and interests. To maximize the potential of each learner, you will need to adapt lessons so that each student can acquire knowledge and skills and feel that he or she is an appreciated member of your learning community.

✓ Each of us has multifaceted learning capacities. We have talents in some areas and difficulties in other areas. The materials and methods you use to teach the curriculum can either present barriers to learning or enhance students' opportunities to acquire knowledge and skills. Your challenge is to understand how the students you teach learn and to design lessons that help everyone learn more effectively.

Employ Graphic Organizers

You don't understand anything until you learn it more than one way.

—Marvin Minsky, American scientist in
the field of artificial intelligence

"How can I help students understand how concepts are related?"

"How can I introduce lessons in an interesting manner?"

"How can I help students remember important facts?"

"How can we review what we previously discussed?"

"How can I actively involve students in summarizing the material they read?"

The answer to each question may be "Use graphic organizers." Graphic organizers—also referred to as networks, webs, visual-spatial displays, graphic representations, semantic organizers, story maps, or concept maps—visually represent a body of knowledge. This can include the critical concepts, vocabulary, events, and/or facts significant to the content taught. Graphic organizers provide a framework to make thought and organization processes visible (Tarquin & Walker, 1997). This framework provides a foundation for learning by linking background knowledge with the major concepts and facts of new learning. Graphic organizers are valuable teaching tools because they help learners to comprehend, summarize, and synthesize complete ideas in ways that, in many instances, surpass verbal statements.

Presented in this section are two examples of graphic organizers. Figure 3.1 is a hierarchical graphic organizer that can be used as an introduction to a unit on good health habits for third-grade students. Figure 3.2 is a sequential graphic organizer for a unit on the digestive system for fourth-grade students.

Graphic organizers allow you to omit extraneous information while emphasizing important concepts and demonstrating their connections to each other. Graphic organizers can show at a glance the key parts of a whole and their relationships, thereby allowing a holistic understanding of the information being presented. At the same time, the lines between terms provide information on the relationships by indicating the connections between concepts and/or facts. This visual representation of information is easier for many students to remember than extended text (Bromley, Irwin-De Vitis, & Modlo, 1995; Dye, 2000). Most importantly, the use of graphic organizers allows students to be actively involved in the processes of listening, speaking, reading, writing, and thinking. As summarized in Figure 3.3 (adapted from Luckner, Bowen, & Carter, 2001), graphic organizers can be created and used in a variety of ways.

Constructing a Graphic Organizer

The construction of the graphic organizer is dictated by the structure of the lesson you want to teach or the materials your students will be reading. Following are four basic patterns:

1. *Hierarchical*—Information that includes a main concept and subconcepts can be organized in a linear manner.

2. *Conceptual*—Information is presented as having a central idea, category, or class with supporting facts, such as characteristics, examples, or descriptors.

Figure 3.1   Hierarchical Graphic Organizer

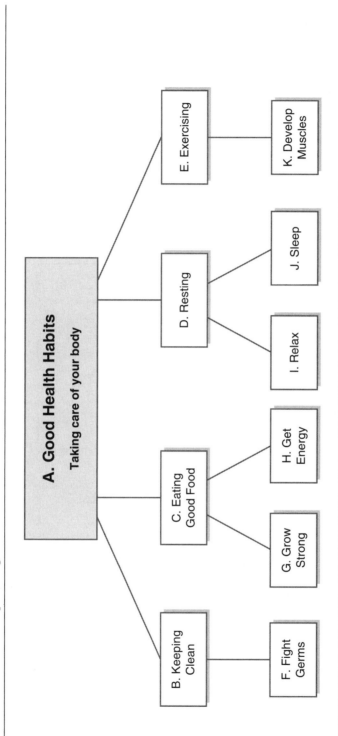

Figure 3.2   Sequential Graphic Organizer of the Digestive System

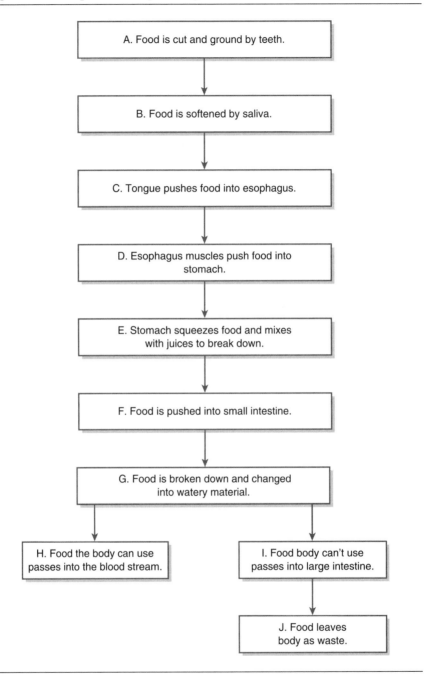

Figure 3.3   Creating and Using Graphic Organizers

Created By	When Created	Purpose of Creation
Teacher	Before students read the material	o To preview reading material, assess prior knowledge, and provide an advanced organizer for content
Teacher	After students have read the material	o To review the reading material, highlighting key points from the chapter o To use as a review or for assessment
Teacher and students	During reading of the material	o To highlight main ideas o To provide assistance for difficult reading passages or concepts
Teacher and students	After students have read the material	o To assess comprehension and outline key points o To use as a review or for assessment
Students	After students have read the material	o To enhance or assess reading comprehension and content information o To review for an examination

3. *Sequential*—The chronological order of events, particularly those having a specific beginning and an end, is displayed. The most common sequential pattern is a time line. However, these patterns also can be used to represent cause/effect, process/ product, or problem/solution situations.

4. *Cyclical*—A series of events that occur within a process can be displayed in a circular formation. There is no beginning or end, just a continuous sequence of events.

To develop a graphic organizer, you can use the following steps. Keep in mind that each graphic organizer can be simplified or made more complex by deleting or adding "branches." This flexibility allows students with different levels of knowledge and skill to participate in the same activity.

1. Determine the concepts and facts you want students to learn.

2. Organize the information in a visual representation that reflects the structure of the content—hierarchical, conceptual, sequential, or cyclical.

3. Prepare a completed graphic organizer. Write in the concepts, vocabulary, definitions, details, events, and facts you want to teach.

4. Include reference points so students can keep their place and follow instructions (i.e., A, B, 1, 2).

5. Make a partially completed organizer that includes the major terms and the actual diagram.

6. Make a blank graphic organizer. Delete all words, leaving only the diagram or structure of the organizer and any added graphics.

Teaching by Using Graphic Organizers

The procedures you use for introducing the graphic organizer will vary, depending on the structure of the organizer you have developed. A graphic organizer can be used to display all of the information that you plan to cover on a topic or only a section of it. Similarly, how you use the graphic organizer will depend on the level of functioning of your students. You may decide to begin the lesson by giving them either a partially or fully completed graphic organizer. By using a partially completed one, the students can fill in the additional information during the lesson. On the other hand, if the students you teach have a great deal of difficulty making written responses, you may decide to give them a completed graphic organizer. When teaching using the graphic organizer, the following is one sequence that you may want to consider:

1. Give a partially completed graphic organizer to students. While you present the lesson, they fill in the new information.

2. Using a computer and projector, an enlarged hard copy, or an overhead transparency, expose the parts of the completed graphic organizer to which you want students to attend.

3. Present each of the concepts, related facts, vocabulary, and examples and nonexamples in a logical order. Stress the relationships between each. Provide examples, definitions, and synonyms for information presented. Ask students questions and have them

generate their own examples as you introduce new parts of the display.

4. At several points during the lesson, review the content and relationships of the graphic organizer prior to adding new information.

5. Check on students' acquisition of the information. Use a partially completed or a blank graphic organizer to conduct a full-class review. Other options include these:

   a. Give a partially completed or a blank graphic organizer to students to work on in small groups or individually.
   b. Have students answer written questions using the organizer as a reference.
   c. Ask students to demonstrate their understanding of material by designing their own graphic organizers for content information.

Inspiration Software Inc. created a pair of valuable software programs, Kidspiration and Inspiration, which can be used for developing graphic organizers. The company allows you to try the software for a 30-day trial period by accessing its Web site: www.inspiration.com.

Bottom Line

✓ Graphic organizers can be used to create visual representations of the overall structure of a lesson or a unit.

✓ When students create their own graphic organizers, they focus on how concepts relate to one another and can see how new concepts are related to things they already know.

✓ The process of having students construct graphic organizers helps them encode information into long-term memory.

Use Learning Centers

Real learning is always about answering a question or solving a problem.

—Charles Handy, Irish business innovator and cofounder of the London Business School

Learning centers are designated areas of the classroom where students engage in specific activities to facilitate learning. While many teachers think of using learning centers with young students, learning centers are appropriate for students of all ages. Learning centers can take many forms and be used to augment instruction in almost all academic areas. Depending on how they are set up, structured, and managed, learning centers are beneficial because they provide opportunities for the following:

- Concrete, hands-on experiences
- Variety in the classroom
- Individualized instruction
- Learning through various modes
- Alternatives to pencil-and-paper seatwork
- Students to work at their own rate
- Development of self-discipline
- Immediate self-evaluation
- Students to work collaboratively
- Extra help and practice

The learning center can parallel classroom instruction, encourage exploration, reinforce a curriculum area, provide a framework for a theme with curricular linkages, or provide enrichment experiences and activities. Three types of learning centers that you may want to consider using are skills centers, discovery or enrichment centers, and creativity centers. The following is a brief explanation of each:

1. *Skills center*—A skills center can include activities such as a listening to recorded books, independent reading, vocabulary games, math facts practice, handwriting practice, word searches, writing book reviews, grammar practice, or solving math word problems.

2. *Discovery or enrichment center*—This center might include science activities, brainteasers, short videos, WebQuests, or advanced mathematics activities.

3. *Creativity center*—This center may include art, crafts, mathematics, or language arts activities, such as journal writing or a class Web page.

Setting Up the Learning Center

You will want to introduce the center in such a way that the students fully understand the directions and how to use the materials, activities, and media available. Evaluation procedures and how materials are to be returned should also be explained before students begin using the center. If you carefully demonstrate the use of the center and periodically monitor its use, many problems can be avoided.

One of the most common problems associated with learning centers is the time it may take to develop them. Initially, development does take extra time and effort, but once the learning centers are produced, they can be easily modified and used in subsequent years. You may want to have students help set up the center, or you may ask a paraprofessional, parent, or volunteer to help.

Learning centers have several essential components, which will vary, depending on the purpose of the center and the age of the students you teach. Each learning center should have clearly stated objectives that structure the activities. Understandable directions should be provided that specify what should be done, where and which materials should be used, and how the work will be evaluated. Design of the center itself includes furniture arrangement (or lack of it), student materials, and the method of presentation (e.g., task cards, computer, microscopes, art supplies, and/or a combination of the available resources). Methods of student response and additional materials that you will require also need to be considered. The following are steps to address when setting up learning centers:

1. Determine the educational goals and purposes the center will serve.

2. Specify your objectives.

3. Choose the optimum space and decide upon a design for the center.

   a. How much space can be allocated to the center?
   b. Does the center need certain environmental conditions (e.g., plants in a science center need to be near light or windows)?

4. Secure needed furniture and materials.

5. Design the learning activities.

   a. Are the activities consistent with the objectives of the center?
   b. Is there a wide assortment of activities to accommodate varying abilities, learning styles, and interests?

6. Write instructions for the students' use of the center.

7. Devise a management system.

8. Set up the center.

9. Orient students to the center.

10. Evaluate the center.

Organizing and Maintaining Learning Centers

- Begin with one learning center in an area of personal strength (e.g., reading, writing, computers, math, science) or in an area especially interesting to you and the students you teach.
- Create a storage system of boxes, file folders, or large envelopes. Label all of the materials in each storage container.
- Plan the year with another teacher who is interested in rotating centers and sharing materials.
- Set a time schedule for using the centers.
- Supply and resupply the necessary materials for each activity.
- Provide a record sheet listing the activities and have students record those they complete.
- Periodically add new activities to an existing center or create a completely new center.
- Consider developing activities that are self-checking so you can reduce the amount of paperwork you need to complete. Examples include answer keys and audiocassettes of correct answers.
- Take photos of the centers to help you remember how to set them up in the future.

Bottom Line

✓ Students learn in diverse ways. Using learning centers honors those differences and provides students with varied ways to interact with content material.

✓ Learning centers provide an avenue for students to practice, explore, apply newly learned skills, be creative, and interact with their classmates. While the initial design and arrangement of a learning center requires additional time and effort, most educators who incorporate learning centers into their teaching repertoire consider them very worthwhile.

Incorporate Activities

To be playful and serious at the same time is possible, and it defines the ideal mental condition.

—John Dewey (1859–1952), American philosopher, psychologist, and educational reformer

Activities are valuable for two reasons. First, appropriately selected and structured activities provide opportunities for students to remember and master the content being taught. Success with practice activities helps students learn (Ormrod, 2008). Second, after sitting and attending for a prolonged block of time, it is easy for students to become restless and distracted. Short breaks that include an activity will help students become more attentive and focused on the content to be learned. In this section, a variety of activities are introduced. Most can be adapted to the content you want to practice, as well as to the age of the students you teach. Also, Resources in the back of this book provides many URLs where you can access activities, games, and practice material.

- *Choral responding*—You ask a review or practice question, and the students either answer simultaneously on a cue from you, turn to their neighbors and tell them the answer, or write down the answer and then compare responses with their neighbors'.

- *Response cards*—You ask a review or practice question, and on cue, students hold up their cards or signs or give the thumbs-up or thumbs-down signal. True/false or yes/no questions are most appropriate for this activity.

- *Memory*—Create cards with a vocabulary or important concept on one card and a definition or explanation on a matching card.

- *Jeopardy*—Ask students to create answers and questions related to the content being studied that could be used as a quiz. Have small groups play a simulated game of Jeopardy using the content area answers and questions.

- *Adapted board games*—Let students play standard board games (e.g., Bingo, Candy Land, Parcheesi, Sorry, Trivial Pursuit) using academic content you have created matched to the curriculum material you want students to learn.

- *Hangman*—Choose spelling words or content vocabulary to be guessed. Draw a picture of the gallows, write the letters of the alphabet across the top of the board or paper, and make a dash for each letter of the word. Players guess a letter of the alphabet. If it is one of the letters of the chosen word, the letter is written on the correct dash. If it appears more than once, it is written on all the appropriate dashes. If it is an incorrect letter, that letter is crossed off on the top of the board or paper, and one piece of a stick figure is drawn just below the gallows. With each incorrect guess, the letter is crossed out and another body part is added. The body parts to add include head, neck, arms (one at a time), hands (one at a time), body, legs (one at a time), and feet (one at a time). The object is for students to guess the word before the stick figure is fully drawn.

- *Fact or opinion*—Students often have a challenging time differentiating between fact and opinion. Before starting, provide an explicit, "student-friendly" definition of the terms *fact* and *opinion* and a few examples and nonexamples for each. Then provide statements such as those listed below for students to respond to. You can call on individual students or have everyone choral respond with thumbs-up = fact, thumbs-down = opinion.
  - o The sun rises in the east (fact).
  - o The moon travels around the earth (fact).
  - o Colorado is a wonderful place to live (opinion).
  - o The Internet is one of the greatest inventions of all time (opinion).

- *Big words*—Write a long word on the board and have the students form as many smaller words as possible using only the letters of that word. For example, if you wrote the word *experiment* on the board, students could identify the words *mint, pen, term, pint, ten, rim, mere, time, rent, mine, tin, men, it, prime, tire, net, ripe,* and *mix*.

- *Add one more*—Have students take out a piece of paper and list as many items that would fit in the category you identify in a one- or two-minute period. Alternatively, state the category and have students raise their hands and share items they think fit in the category you designate. Examples of prompts include these:
  - o Words that rhyme with _____
  - o Animals that live on a farm, in the water, at the zoo, etc.
  - o Things that have handles

- o Nouns
- o Verbs
- o Adjectives
- o Prepositional phrases
- o Names of fruits, vegetables, meats
- o Names of countries in Europe
- o Names of states and their capitals
- o Types of sports
- o Musical instruments
- o Famous explorers
- o Occupations

• *Doesn't belong*—Read a group of four or five words and have students identify which one doesn't belong. Examples include the following:

- o Dog, cat, camel, gerbil; answer = camel—not a pet
- o Toes, girl, knee, ear; answer = girl—not a body part
- o Dolphin, monkey, whale, octopus; answer = monkey—not an aquatic animal
- o Peanut butter, jelly, bread, olives; answer = bread—not stored in a jar
- o Openness, stealth, covert, secret; answer = openness—not a word describing slyness

• *Analogies*—Often students need instruction and practice in seeing the relationship between two items (e.g., foot and toe) and then generalizing that connection to another set of items (e.g., hand and finger). Provide sufficient explanations and practice activities and then share some items similar to those listed below:

- o *German shepherd* is to *dog* as a *parakeet* is to _____ (bird).
- o *Tennis* is to *racquet* as *baseball* is to _____ (bat).
- o *Bacon* is to a *pig* as a *hamburger* is to _____ (cow).
- o *Scales* are to *fish* as _____ is to *humans* (skin).

• *Idioms*—Many students have not been exposed to the idioms that they encounter when reading. Have students explain the meaning of idioms similar to those listed below:

- o Cold feet
- o Rat race
- o All thumbs
- o A stick in the mud
- o Second thoughts
- o Keep it under your hat
- o In a pickle

o Chip on his shoulder
o Too many irons in the fire
o When pigs fly
o Nose to the grindstone
o Chomping at the bit

• *Similes*—As with analogies and idioms, students need exposure to and practice with similes. Begin with easy and common similes, and as students become more skilled, increase the difficulty and suggest that they create more unusual similes. Here are a few examples:

o Stinky as a _____ (skunk, sweaty sock)
o Quiet as a _____ (whisper, butterfly)
o Swift as a _____ (shooting star, race car)

• *Acronyms*—Acronyms are words formed by the initials or other parts of several words. They are used daily in conversation and in newspapers and magazines. Help students learn what the initials stand for. Here are a few to get you started:

o WWW = World Wide Web
o CNN = Cable News Network
o SUV = sports utility vehicle
o PIN = personal identification number
o COP = constable on patrol
o EPA = Environmental Protection Agency
o EENT = eyes, ears, nose, and throat
o GPS = Global Positioning System
o Hazmat = hazardous material
o FAQ = frequently asked questions
o FEMA = Federal Emergency Management Agency
o DNF = did not finish
o ESPN = Entertainment & Sports Programming Network
o CD-ROM = compact disc—read only memory
o Yuppie = young urban professional
o HMO = health maintenance organization
o Moped = motorized pedal cycle
o 4-H = head, heart, hands, and health
o VCR = videocassette recorder
o Scuba = self-contained underwater breathing apparatus
o Tips = to improve personal service

• *Graph it*—There are a variety of ways to indicate relationships between two or more variables. Practice using graphs, histograms, pie charts, and tables can be fun if you use some interesting student data to make the graphs. Examples include the following:

- o Month of birthday
- o Shoe size
- o Favorite food
- o Color of hair
- o Favorite sport
- o Favorite singer
- o Favorite television show

• *Spell it: Last letter is now the first*—Say a word and then spell it out loud. Then point to a student, who must use the last letter of the word you spelled as the first letter of a word that he or she must spell before you count to 5. That student spells the word and then points to another student, who must use the last letter of the word his or her classmate spelled as the first letter of a word that he or she spells. Here is an example:

1. You say and spell elephan*t.*
2. First student says and spells *tiger.*
3. Second student says and spells *ring.*
4. Third student says and spells *gem.*

• *Draw it*—Help students improving their listening and following directions skills. First, take a moment and create a drawing that includes shapes at different places on a piece of paper. Then, pass out unlined paper. Without showing students your drawing, ask them to listen as you describe it. Then have them draw, trying to come as close as possible to matching your drawing. Here is an example of the directions:

- o In the middle of the paper, draw a rectangle.
- o Write your name in the rectangle.
- o Below the rectangle, draw a triangle.
- o Inside the triangle, draw a circle.
- o On top of the rectangle, draw a square.
- o Divide the square in half.
- o Put dots in the left-hand side of the square.
- o Put a star in the upper right-hand corner of the paper.
- o In the bottom left-hand corner of the paper, draw two squares.
- o Put an X inside the second square.

• *Going on a trip*—You start by saying, "I'm going on a trip and I'm taking a _____." You name an item that you would take on a trip, such as a shirt. Then you point to a student, who says, "I'm going on a trip, and I'm taking a shirt and a _____." The student repeats the previous statement and adds another item, such as a pair of shoes. This process continues, with students repeating what they heard and adding an item until a mistake is made. Alternatives include "I'm going to the zoo, and I am going to see _____," "I'm going to the grocery store, and I'll buy _____," "I'm going to the airport, and I'm going to see _____," "I'm going to a place we are studying (e.g., Alaska), and I'm going to see _____," or "I'm taking a time machine to a point in the past or future (e.g., the 1920s), and I see _____."

Bottom Line

✓ Students benefit from a short break of a minute or two to get up and stretch their bodies or an opportunity to stretch their minds and do an invigorating activity. Additionally, the class frequently has a few extra minutes before lunch, prior to the end of the day, or just before getting ready to change classes. Activities such as those listed above can be used to reinforce important concepts and facts, as well as to energize students.

✓ Practice and energizer activities do not have to be competitive. They also can be designed to optimize cooperation.

4

Teaching Effectively Part III

Helping Students Benefit From Assessment

Assess and Monitor Students' Progress

Life is like a combination lock; your job is to find the right numbers, in the right order, so you can have anything you want.

—Brian Tracy,
Canadian-American motivational author

Good teaching requires an appropriate balance of assessment and instruction. To ensure that the students you work with are learning and that you are providing appropriate instruction, you will need to gather information of different types over time. Stiggins (2005) estimates that you will spend a quarter to a third of your time involved in assessment-related activities. This includes development, selection from other sources, administration, scoring, reviewing, recording, and reporting results. While this may seem like a large percentage of your time, research (e.g., Black, Harrison, Lee, Marshall, & William, 2004; Black & William, 1998; Meisels, Atkins-Burnett, Xue, & Bickel, 2003) suggests that this is time well spent; that is, when teachers take the time to identify student needs and conduct continuous formative assessments about students' mastery of specified material, positive achievement increases. At the same time, inaccurate assessments often lead to misidentification of student needs; failure to understand which instructional strategies are effective and which are not; and communication of misinformation to colleagues, families, and students.

While the process of assessment allows you to collect data on students so you can make informed decisions, assessment data have also become increasingly important to curriculum specialists, administrators, school boards, families, and public officials. They want to verify that students are meeting academic standards and that they are prepared to participate in our information-based society. As a result, we see an increase in the use of standardized tests and statewide assessments to inform interested parties about how students are performing. These tests are often referred to as "high-stakes tests" because important decisions about students' educational programs, such as promotion and graduation, are made based on the test results.

Though these forms of evaluation are important parts of our contemporary education system, concerns have been raised about relying on one exam as the measurement of student learning (e.g., Amrein & Berliner, 2003). In addition, these tests are of limited instructional value to teachers because they only occur once a year, they are broad in focus, and the results are not returned in timely manner so that teachers can use them to make day-to-day decisions (Stiggins, 2005). As a result, the focus of this section is on classroom assessments that provide a continuous flow of evidence of student mastery of classroom-level learning targets, leading over time to the attainment of desired achievement standards. Information on other forms of assessment is discussed in the next section, "Prepare for State and District Assessments."

Teacher-Made Tests

To help you evaluate students' performance and to make decisions about the effectiveness of your instruction, you will create tests and/or use all of or parts of assessments provided by curriculum developers. The most important factor is the test content. You will need to be certain that the content of the test items is directly related to your instruction and that the vocabulary and concepts that appear on the test are consistent with those that have been used in class.

The second most important factor to consider is the test format. Specific pitfalls you want to avoid include (1) unclear directions,

(2) ambiguous statements, (3) complex phrasing, and (4) difficult vocabulary (Popham, 2003). Preferably, tests should be word processed, properly spaced, and printed with a large enough font size so students can easily read the material. Providing directions on the same page as the items, allowing students to write on the test itself rather than transferring answers to a separate page, and providing sufficient space for each response helps students focus on the content of the test.

Tests can include selected-response items (e.g., true-false, matching, multiple-choice) and/or constructed-response items (e.g., short-answer, essay). Selected-response items tend to be best for assessing students' knowledge of factual information, while constructed-response items tend to require students to analyze and synthesize information. Selected-response items are easier and faster to score, but they don't require students to generate their own answers. Constructed-response items allow students to use their own words to demonstrate their understanding, but they take more time to score and the scoring may be less precise than for selected-response items.

Guidelines for writing selected-response items include the following:

1. Try to avoid using categorical words, such as *never, always,* or *all.*

2. Include only one major point in each item.

3. When using matching, limit each section to no more than ten items.

4. Avoid asking students to draw lines from one column to another. Instead provide a blank and have students record the number or letter of the matching selection in a blank space you have provided.

5. When using multiple-choice questions, avoid using "all of the above" as an answer choice.

6. When using matching questions, place all items on the same page so students don't have to flip back and forth between pages to respond.

7. When using multiple-choice questions, be sure that each answer choice is grammatically consistent with the stem of the item.

Guidelines for writing constructed-response items include the following:

1. When using short-answer items, use direct questions rather than incomplete statements.

2. When using sentence completion items, try to place the blank near the end of the item, require only one word or a short phrase, and try not to include more than one blank per item.

3. Essay questions should be written in a manner that is appropriate for students' reading level.

4. Phrase essay questions as precisely as possible so that students understand specifically to what aspect of the content or issue they should respond.

5. When using essays, use more questions requiring short answers rather than fewer questions requiring longer responses.

Progress Monitoring

Progress monitoring has been defined as "frequent and ongoing measurement of student knowledge and skills and the examination of student data to evaluate instruction" (Vaughn, Bos, & Schumm, 2007, p. 74). Progress monitoring is used to keep track of students' learning, to identify students who need additional help, to assist in arranging small-group instruction, and to design instruction that meets individual needs. Progress monitoring can be implemented with an entire class or with individual students.

To implement progress monitoring, the students' current levels of performance on specific skills (e.g., word identification fluency, passage reading fluency, computation, spelling) are determined, and goals are identified for learning that will take place over time. The steps often undertaken for conducting progress monitoring, adapted from Fuchs, Fuchs, and Powell (2004), are as follows:

1. *Decide on level of implementation* (i.e., individual student, small group, classroom, grade level, school level, district level).

2. *Decide what measures to use.* Create or select appropriate tests/probes. They should sample skills to be mastered across the school year and generally be one to two minutes in duration.

3. *Collect screening or baseline data.* Administer and score the tests/probes. Probes are presented frequently (e.g., weekly or monthly) to ensure that students' data are valid and reliable.

4. *Decide on short-term objectives or end criteria.*

5. *Set long-range goals.* Targets, which sometimes are called benchmarks, help students and teachers understand how much growth is expected and required.

6. *Decide how often to monitor.*

7. *Graph the scores.* Visual representations of students' performance enable students to see their progress and teachers to make instructional decisions.

8. *Make instructional decisions.* The students' performance is used to evaluate the instructional program to retain effective strategies and to discontinue ineffective ones.

9. *Continue monitoring.*

10. *Communicate progress.* The data and graphs facilitate communication with parents, other teachers, and students.

A variety of commercial progress-monitoring assessment systems (e.g., AIMSweb, Edcheckup), as well as free materials (e.g., Curriculum-Based Measurement Warehouse), is available. In addition, many textbook publishers provide materials that can be used for progress monitoring. See Resources in the back of this book for additional information.

Performance Assessment

Performance assessments require students to demonstrate certain skills or to create products that exhibit their ability to apply knowledge and skills. Examples of performance assessments are producing writing samples, orally reading a passage from a book, participating in a debate, developing a brochure about proper nutrition, keyboarding, or painting a picture. The advantage of using performance assessment is that students are actively involved in tasks in which they must demonstrate their mastery of processes and/or develop authentic products. One potential disadvantage of performance assessments is that they tend to be time consuming in their development as well as in the demonstration of the performance. A second possible drawback of performance assessment is the requirement to develop evaluation criteria for the performance and to apply the evaluation criteria objectively to the performance.

Portfolios

A portfolio is a systematic and organized collection of work that has been assembled over time to monitor a student's growth. Following are reasons that you may want to use portfolios:

- Portfolios have intrinsic interest to teachers and students because they link the assessment and teaching process by directly tying together student efforts and learning objectives.
- Assessment is a multidimensional process whereby the portfolio may contain several samples of student work assembled in a purposeful manner with pieces representing work in progress as well as showpiece samples.
- Portfolios provide an avenue for continuous and systematic assessment, which helps students, teachers, and parents to see what students are actually learning, the skills being developed and the problems occurring, and to create appropriate goals.
- Using portfolios permits opportunities for students to be reflective about their work, thereby making the process of assessment a shared endeavor between teachers and students.

The primary challenges of using portfolios are time and the fact that portfolios are a labor-intensive process. Time needs to be devoted to develop, review, and present the portfolios.

As you begin considering how to use portfolios, it is important to think about five aspects of the portfolio: the purpose, the physical format, the artifact selection, the procedures for storing the portfolio, and the procedures for evaluating the portfolio.

1. *Purpose*—The most important initial step is to determine the purpose for the portfolio. In general, the purpose or goals of the portfolio are related directly to the curriculum that will be covered over an extended period of time (e.g., a unit, a trimester, the school year).

2. *Physical format*—The two aspects of the physical format to consider are the way materials are organized and the presentation or packaging of the entire portfolio. An accordion folder, a box, or three-ring notebooks with pocketed dividers are three common ways to collect products.

3. *Selection of artifacts*—This is generally the most motivating part of the portfolio process. Careful thought needs to be given to

what materials can provide the best evidence of student growth. The following are examples of portfolio items:

o Writing drafts from prewriting through completed piece, with prompts and scoring criteria

o Science log pages, which demonstrate the ability to conduct, do analysis upon, and interpret lab experiments

o A compact disk or videotape of a student presentation, demonstration, or investigation

o Photographs of products and projects as they evolved, accompanied by the student's reflective statements

o A recording of an oral reading from a chapter in a book

o Special awards, recognitions, and certificates

4. *Storage*—Portfolios should be stored in an area in the classroom that is easily accessible to you and the students you teach. Availability invites students to contribute to the portfolio on an ongoing basis and permits opportunities for reflection and planning future learning opportunities.

5. *Evaluation*—The last step is to review, evaluate, and—whenever possible—share the portfolios with others. When feasible, evaluation criteria should be established in advance and explained to students before they begin work on their portfolios. Also, you will need to decide whether you will be evaluating the entire portfolio or distinct portfolio entries.

Rubrics

A rubric is a printed set of scoring guidelines that provide explicit information about the types of performances you expect students to demonstrate on tests, assignments, or projects. Most often, rubrics consist of a simple grid containing aspects of a task or situation on one axis (e.g., for a general writing rubric, the characteristics might be Introduction/Conclusion, Organization, Content, and Structural Quality) and, on the other, the levels of achievement with descriptive criteria for each level. Criteria might be Beginning, Developing, Accomplished, Exemplary or numerical scores (e.g., 1, 2, 3, and 4), whose sum is associated with a grade.

Benefits of rubrics include the following:

- The desired standards of performance are defined.
- Descriptive feedback is provided to students about how they can improve.

- Students can be involved in the development of the rubric and/or self-assessment.
- An avenue for teacher-student communication is available.

Although the construction of rubrics generally takes additional time, they typically simplify the grading process. Also, if you give students a rubric before they begin an assignment, it will help them see exactly how you will assess their work. Figure 4.1 is an example of a rubric you could use to evaluate reports written by students. See Resources in the back of this book for Web sites that provide suggestions for constructing rubrics, as well as other forms of rubrics that can be downloaded and used.

Figure 4.1   Sample Rubric for Expository Writing Project

Traits	Criterion			
	Excellent	*Average*	*Below Average*	*Unacceptable*
Content Knowledge	Author demonstrates strong understanding of the topic.	Author is at ease with content but fails to provide sufficient detail.	Author is uncomfortable with topic and is unable to explain basic concepts.	Author does not demonstrate a basic understanding of the topic.
Organization	Information is logical and very easy to follow.	Most of the information is presented in a logical sequence that the reader can follow.	Reader has difficulty following meaning because author jumps around.	Sequence of information is very difficult to follow.
Conventions	Work has no misspellings, grammatical errors, or punctuation errors.	Work has a small number of misspellings, grammatical errors, and/or punctuation errors.	Work has some misspellings, grammatical errors, and/or punctuation errors.	Work has a large number of misspellings, grammatical errors, and/or punctuation errors.

Checklists

Checklists can be used to observe and record a list of characteristics or behaviors (e.g., oral reading, math facts, spelling words, off-task behavior, and homework completion). You can use existing checklists, create your own checklists, or tailor available checklists to the developmental level of the students you teach and/or the specific items on which you want to focus. When developing checklists, consider the following guidelines, adapted from Cohen and Spenciner (2003):

- Keep items brief.
- Subject and verb tense should be consistent (e.g., "Reads expressively. Uses context cues.").
- Stress positive behaviors—emphasize what students can do.
- Do not repeat items.
- Arrange items in the order you expect them to occur.
- Use a system for indicating when a characteristic or behavior occurs (e.g., checkmark, yes or no, plus or minus sign).
- Include a space for a comment or description if appropriate.

Bottom Line

✓ The primary purpose of assessment is to promote more effective classroom instruction.

✓ Effective teachers assess the students they work with in a variety of ways throughout the school year.

✓ Classroom assessment conducted well and regularly has demonstrated positive gains in student achievement.

✓ Shorter, more frequent tests may be more beneficial to students and to you than longer, more comprehensive tests.

✓ All forms of classroom assessment have strengths and limitations. Being aware of the specific purpose of the assessment will help you determine the type of assessment to use.

Prepare for State and District Assessments

Our progress as a nation can be no swifter than our progress in education. The human mind is our fundamental resource.

—John F. Kennedy (1917–1963), U.S. president

Assessment has always been an integral component of the education process. However, recently the essential role of assessment methods, instruments, and processes and the use of results have become increasingly important to the education community as well as to the general public.

In the 1980s, the social mission of schools began to change. A push for schools to increase academic standards as well as a focusing of attention on the attainment of life skills and job-related competencies began. As a result, over the last couple of decades, the emphasis on effective schools has increased; today, education stakeholders expect that all students will leave school having met a minimum level of competence in a variety of academic areas.

With higher expectations for students' performance, the role of assessment expanded. The frequency of classroom assessments increased, and the types of assessments that educators used also changed. In addition to the end-of-unit paper-and-pencil tests, educators increasingly assessed students' attitudes, knowledge, and skills using portfolios, projects, and performances. Simultaneously, another change that affected schools was the development and implementation of academic content standards and performance standards.

- *Academic content standards* are statements of the subject-specific knowledge and skills that teachers should teach and students should know and be able to do in various subject areas at different stages of schooling.
- *Performance standards* are statements to describe the proficiency with which students will show that they have mastered the academic content standards.

These changes have resulted in educators spending larger blocks of time assessing students' performance based on criteria closely aligned with academic content and performance standards. These, in turn, have been aligned with, as well as translated into, state assessments in which students participate annually.

The increased use of state assessments has occurred as a result of the No Child Left Behind Act (NCLB) being signed into law to provide a framework for improving the performance of America's elementary and secondary schools. One of the principles of this act is stronger accountability for results. Accountability refers to "the use of assessment results and other data to ensure that schools are moving in desired directions" (Salvia & Ysseldyke, 2006, p. 657). Consequently, school districts must annually assess students in Grades 3 through 8 and once in Grades 10 through 12 to determine whether students are making "adequate yearly progress" in meeting state-determined standards in reading, mathematics, and science. Students with significant disabilities may be given alternative assessments, but they must show improvement commensurate with their ability levels.

NCLB also requires that school districts report on the participation and performance of students on their state assessments. The assessment results are made available to educators, families, and students to examine progress of student mastery of the standards. In turn, federal, state, and local policy makers, as well as the general public, use the assessment results to judge if schools and/or school districts are effective or not. Schools that demonstrate progress receive awards (such as teacher bonuses, increased budgets, and special recognition for having a large percentage of students meeting a particular assessment performance level). Schools that do not show improvement are subject to sanctions and corrective actions (assigning negative labels to schools, removing staff, firing principals), and students have the option of attending a better public school at the school district's expense. In some states, the scores on state assessments are also being used to make decisions about whether a student will move from one grade to another or receive a standard high school diploma or some other type of document.

While most educators agree with the intent of NCLB—to boost students' academic achievement—many have expressed dissatisfaction about how the law has been implemented. Specific concerns often cited include the following:

- Students with disabilities and English-language learners who previously were not included in such assessments are not prepared for these tests. The education they were receiving was geared to their special needs (e.g., supplementary help with reading and math, bilingual education instruction) rather than the content upon which state assessments are founded.
- Nationally, there is no consensus on educational standards. Consequently, the academic content and performance standards, as well as what is established as "adequate yearly progress," varies from state to state.
- High standards for performance may be unrealistic for students who may have had poor nutrition and little preparation for academic work prior to their school years.
- Teachers are unable to teach content material in depth because the amount of information to be covered can be daunting. In addition, many of the assessments focus on factual knowledge rather than process and application skills.

- Some students don't see the value of the tests; as a result, they have little motivation to put forth their best effort, therefore providing significant underestimates of what they have learned.
- Some students are dropping out of school, either because they performed poorly on a state assessment or because they fear failing one.

Standards-based reform efforts and NCLB have significantly affected our current educational system. Undoubtedly, questions about how academic standards are set, measured, and reported, as well as how schools are going to meet some of the additional aspects of the law not discussed here, will continue to be raised for years to come as policies are created, litigation occurs, and the legislation is revised. Hopefully, the primary focus will turn to supporting and rewarding effective instructional practice while simultaneously increasing test scores.

Using State and District Assessments

The background information presented in this section was provided because you will have to wrestle with the ethical as well as the practical issues of state and district assessments and determine your own personal stance. Clearly, this is a controversial issue that is not likely to disappear in the near future. Consequently, you can take specific actions to help yourself and the students you teach gain the maximum benefit from participating in state and district assessments.

- As you begin the process of designing a course of study, the foundation of the lesson plan should be your state standards. Plan lessons with mastery of the state standards as your objective because they will be the indicator of your students' success.
- Reduce test anxiety. Be positive and encouraging to students before, during, and after the assessments. Send notes home to families about the importance of proper sleep and nutrition to help students be physically prepared for the tests.
- Help students perform well on tests. Integrate the information included in some of the other sections of this text (e.g., "Attend to the Science of Teaching" and "Increase Academic Learning Time" in Chapter 2, "Teach Study Skills" and "Instruct Students on How to Pass Tests" later in this chapter) so that you provide quality classroom instruction that helps students learn.

- Take the time to familiarize yourself with the state and district tests the students you teach will take. Provide students with practice on the kinds of test items they will experience when they take the assessments.
- Help students and families understand the tests. Assessment scores can be very confusing. It is important for you to understand what the different types of scores mean and do not mean, because it will be your responsibility to explain them to families and sometimes to students themselves. Examples of concepts/ terms you will want to become familiar with include *standards, domains, raw scores, cutoff score, percentile score* or *percentile rank, stanine, confidence band,* and *grade equivalent scores.* In some districts, you will also have to explain the specific connection between scores on the test and grade retention and graduation.
- Become familiar with the assessment accommodations available for students with disabilities. Accommodations refer to any change in testing materials or procedures that enables students to participate in assessments so that their abilities, rather than their disabilities, are assessed. Following are the five general types of accommodations and examples of each:
  1. *Presentation*—Braille, sign language, recording of directions, having test read aloud, extra examples
  2. *Setting*—Separate room, study carrel, special lighting, seat near test administrator
  3. *Schedule*—Over several days, at a specific time of day
  4. *Response*—Mark response in booklet, use word processor, point to answer
  5. *Timing*—Extended time, frequent breaks, multiple days

  In general, accommodations used for testing should be the same as the accommodations used during instruction, as listed on the student's individualized education program (IEP).

- Maintain perspective about the type of information the tests provide. Communicate to families the importance of keeping these tests in perspective. State and district tests help answer specific questions, such as "How do the students in this class, grade, school, or district compare with other students in this class, grade, school, or district in specific content areas?" While you may have different pressing questions, such as "Are students learning the content material? Am I going too fast or too slow? Did that teaching strategy work? Which students need extra help?" it is important to keep in mind that different forms of assessment answer different questions. Consequently, you should be aware of the questions you want to and/or need to answer and be knowledgeable about the appropriate assessment method useful in gathering data to answer each question.

Bottom Line

✓ Good classroom instruction is the best way to help students grow as learners and perform well on state and district assessments.

✓ State and district assessments provide information that many individuals feel is important. However, your classroom assessments will have a much larger impact on student learning, because the once-a-year assessments do not provide you with the moment-to-moment, day-to-day, and week-to-week information about students that you need to make important instructional decisions. Use both forms of assessment to make evaluations about what is best for the students you teach.

Teach Study Skills

The object of education is to prepare the young to educate themselves throughout their lives.

—Robert M. Hutchins (1899–1977),
American educational philosopher

Study skills are essential for all students to succeed in school, as well as when they leave school. In actuality, each of us uses a variety of study skills on a daily basis (e.g., self-management, organization, time management, summarizing, and comprehension monitoring). Consequently, many researchers and learning theorists suggest that schools should provide explicit instruction in how to study and learn (e.g., Ormrod, 2008; Siegler & Alibali, 2005). However, instruction in study skills does not occur often enough because teachers assume that students learn these skills on their own, have mastered them at an earlier level, or that students know enough about their own learning to be able to generalize strategies across academic content areas

(Harvey, 2002). Unfortunately, these assumptions are often incorrect. Fortunately, research has demonstrated that all learners, even those as young as four years old, can be taught effective learning and study strategies that lead to improvements in their memory, classroom performance, and academic achievement (e.g., Fletcher & Bray, 1996; Hattie, Biggs, & Purdie, 1996).

Study skills include those competencies associated with acquiring, recording, remembering, organizing, synthesizing, and using information and ideas (Polloway, Patton, & Serna, 2005). As students move up through the grades, the learning tasks they are required to do become progressively more complex. Specifically, as students advance from elementary school to high school, they are expected to remember more information, understand information at a more abstract level, and be able to use the information to complete higher-level thinking operations.

To become effective learners, individuals need to become intentional and strategic—they need to be actively and consciously engaged in the process of learning. While some learning is unconscious and automatic, the vast majority of learning in our information-based society requires attention, self-regulation, and strategic use of cognitive and metacognitive (i.e., thinking about thinking) processes (Langer, 2000). Unfortunately, many students don't consistently use effective study strategies. Reasons include the following (Ormrod, 2008; Rauch & Fillenworth, 1995):

- Students have never been taught how to study successfully.
- Students mistakenly believe they already use effective strategies.
- Students are overwhelmed by the quantity of material teachers expect them to master, so they spend time getting the general idea rather than really trying to understand it.
- Students believe they already know the material.
- Students erroneously think using study strategies requires too much time and effort.
- Students are not interested in learning for understanding and, as a result, want to expend as little time and/or effort as possible.

Helping Students Develop Effective Study Strategies

You can undertake a variety of strategies to help students master new knowledge and skills. The following recommendations focus on methods for organizing instruction and for promoting the development of students' studying skills to remember and learn information (Ormrod, 2008; Pashler et al., 2007):

- Teach study strategies using the academic content being taught in class. Suggest how students can organize their notes, provide mnemonics for material that is difficult to remember (e.g., HOMES for the five Great Lakes, ROY G. BIV for the colors of the spectrum), and ask students to summarize the content that has recently been presented.
- Model effective study strategies by thinking aloud about new material. By thinking out loud about the content your class is studying and describing some of the strategies you have found effective to remember content, you help the students to see how you organize and process information effectively.
- Require students to develop sets of flash cards that include key vocabulary, concept explanations, formulas, or procedures. Have students review them with a peer at the beginning or end of a lesson several times a week prior to the end of the unit test.
- Combine graphics with verbal descriptions. As explained in the section in Chapter 3 titled "Employ Graphic Organizers," research indicates that adding relevant graphical presentations that illustrate key processes and procedures leads to better learning than text and/or verbal descriptions alone.
- Instruction should address procedural strategies (e.g., how to take notes during a lecture, how to highlight material when reading a textbook, how to write summaries), as well as cognitive processes (e.g., predicting what will be read in the next passage, envisioning examples and applications of the material presented).
- Use quizzes to help students practice and recall specific information. Following the initial exposure to the content and prior to the end of the unit test, use short-answer quizzes to help cement the information to memory. Fill-in-the-blank or short-answer type items are better than true/false and multiple-choice items for helping students remember important information longer. Review of the quiz items and corrective feedback should be provided.
- Students should be exposed to a variety of study strategies and practice them with diverse tasks on an ongoing basis. Different strategies are useful in different situations. For example, rehearsal is a good strategy for remembering someone's name, while summarizing is a good strategy for pulling key ideas into a cohesive organizational structure.

- Ask and model responses to higher-level thinking questions to help students build deep explanations of key concepts. Once students have acquired a basic understanding of the topic of study, you can ask questions that require them to respond to questions about causes and consequences, motivations, scientific evidence, and logical justifications. See the section in Chapter 3 titled "Ask Good Questions" for examples of the types of questions that prompt higher-level thinking.

- Allow students to work cooperatively with other students on group learning activities. Because humans are social by nature, students receive multiple benefits when interactions with peers are promoted that are focused on the content to be learned. Peer interaction (a) encourages students to clarify and organize their ideas about the content, (b) provides opportunities for students to expand on what they have learned, (c) exposes students to diverse perspectives on the content, (d) enables students to monitor their comprehension, and (e) can be highly motivating.

Examples of Specific Study Strategies

Following are examples of study strategies you can use to help students meet their educational and life skill needs. Pressley et al. (1995) suggest that you incorporate four elements into your strategy instruction:

1. Introduce the purpose, steps, and procedures for each strategy.

2. Demonstrate how and when to apply each strategy.

3. Provide guided practice and feedback using appropriate materials.

4. Allow students to use each study strategy independently, review their work, and provide feedback.

    - *Organization*—Finding connections within a body of new information and imposing an organizational structure on the information. For students who are not skilled at recognizing the interrelationships in the body of information, you will need to provide direct instruction to help them categorize. By using graphic representations, as well as teaching students to develop their own (such as graphic organizers, flow charts, and time lines), you can help students encode information into long-term memory.

    - *Note taking*—Taking notes on information presented in lectures and textbooks. The process of writing notes helps encode the information. Another benefit of notes is the fact that once they are recorded on paper, they can be reviewed later.

Many students will need to be taught how to write notes in their own words; jot down only critical points, essential details, and examples; and review and edit their notes. You also can help students take better notes by (a) providing a skeletal outline, (b) writing important ideas on the board, and (c) emphasizing important points by repeating them.

- *Summarizing*—Discriminating between important and unimportant information, identifying the main ideas, and organizing critical elements into a cohesive synopsis. Following is a four-step strategy, suggested by Mastropieri and Scruggs (2000), that you can use to help students learn to summarize:

    1. Read a passage or short segment from a book.
    2. Ask yourself who or what the passage is about.
    3. Ask yourself what was happening in the passage.
    4. Make up a summary sentence in your own words using the answers to the questions asked.

- It is best to practice developing summaries with short, easy, well-organized passages and then gradually to introduce more difficult passages. Also, you may want to have students discuss and compare their summaries, so they can see how others have organized the same information.

- *PARS strategy*—A four-step strategy for (1) activating background knowledge; (2) asking questions based on the title, subtitles, pictures, and figures; (3) reading; and (4) summarizing. PARS is an acronym:

    P—Preview.
    A—Ask questions.
    R—Read.
    S—Summarize.

- *RAP Strategy*—A three-step strategy to remember reading material by (1) reading, (2) asking questions, (3) and paraphrasing. RAP is an acronym:

    R—Read the paragraph.
    A—Ask yourself to identify the main idea and two supporting details.
    P—Put main ideas and details into your own words.

- *SQRW Strategy*—A four-step strategy for reading and taking notes from textbooks. Each letter stands for a step in the strategy:

    S—Survey. Read the title, introduction, headings, and summary or conclusion.

Q—Question. Use the words *who, what, where, when, why,* and *how* to change headings into questions. Write the questions on paper.

R—Read. Find the answers to your questions.

W—Write. Write answers to your questions.

Bottom Line

✓ Study skills significantly affect students' ability to function in school. Study skills are often not taught in schools because teachers assume that students already have mastered them. Too often, this is not the case. Study skills can be taught to students of all ages and levels of ability.

✓ Although study skills become increasingly important beginning at the upper elementary level, they initially should be taught to students early in their educational career. Continual practice and instruction should occur throughout elementary, middle, and high school.

✓ For students to become skilled at using study strategies, they will need sufficient modeling and guidance during the early learning phases. Later, they can work more independently as well as cooperatively to apply the study strategies effectively.

Instruct Students on How to Pass Tests

The good teacher makes the poor student good and the good student superior.

—Marva Collins, American educator and
founder of Chicago's Westside Preparatory School

Tests are given frequently in schools to determine how well students have learned specific content area material and to determine overall achievement levels. Many students perform poorly on tests because they lack strategies for taking tests. Providing students with instruction in how to take tests can help them perform better, as well as lessen the anxiety that often accompanies the process of taking tests.

Anxiety and Anxiety Reduction

Anxiety is a feeling of uneasiness and apprehension about a situation. Most of us experience some anxiety when we have to take a test. A small and controllable amount of anxiety is typical, and it actually can help us perform a little better (Cassady & Johnson, 2002). But some students become extremely anxious in test-taking situations, becoming distracted and, as a result, perform poorly.

To help reduce students' anxiety about tests, it is beneficial to encourage students to do their best and not emphasize the consequences of doing poorly. In addition to teaching students the strategies presented below, you can also do the following:

- Provide practice and review opportunities prior to the assessment.
- Teach students study strategies (see the section above titled "Teach Study Skills").
- Use a grading system that includes many data sources rather than one or two test scores (e.g., projects, in-class work, homework, quizzes).
- Tell students what will be covered on the test.
- Let students know what type of test will be given (e.g., multiple-choice, true/false, matching, completion, essay, open-book, open-notes).

Teaching Students Test-Taking Strategies

Many students struggle when taking tests because they do not begin the test in an organized, strategic manner. Examples of strategies you can teach so they can become better test takers on a variety of different types of tests are provided below:

- Many standardized tests require students to record their responses by filling a circle, or "bubble," on a separate answer sheet. Many young students and some older students have difficulty working on two separate forms, especially when the test directions state to not write on the test booklet. As a result, you will want to provide students with practice reading the stimulus question on one form and providing a response on the separate answer form. They should also practice marking their answer dark and inside the lines.
- Learning to budget time to complete the test is very important. Students should be taught to check the time periodically to make sure they have enough time to answer the remaining questions. To help students learn to budget their time, you can

write the remaining time on the board at several points during the testing period.

- On multiple-choice tests, students often hurry through the test, choosing the first item that looks correct without reading all the choices. They should be taught to read all the choices for each question before responding.

- When taking multiple-choice tests and uncertain of the right answer, students can be taught to use the process of elimination to determine the best answer. This strategy involves reading each of the answer choices and eliminating the items they know are incorrect. By getting rid of each item they know is wrong, they reduce the number of possible correct items and increase their chances of selecting the right answer.

- For sentence completion items, those that require students to fill in a blank with a correct answer, students should be encouraged to read the item and think about what is missing. They should write an answer that logically completes the item and then go back and read the entire item to make sure it makes sense as completed. If they are unsure of the right answer, they should put something in the blank, even if the answer is only partly correct, because teachers often give partial credit for some answers.

- When students are working on matching items, you will want to encourage them to read the items on the left-hand column first, then read each choice in the right-hand column before answering. Then they should work on the easiest items prior to attempting the items that are more difficult and cross out items in both columns as they make matches.

- For true-false items, it is helpful to point out that words that moderate a sentence (e.g., *often, usually, many, most, sometimes, generally*) frequently indicate that the statement is true. Also, you will want to explain that a question should only be marked "True" if it is always true.

- Responding to essay test questions is a multistep process. First, students need to underline the word that tells them what to do (e.g., *define, discuss, explain, analyze, describe, list, compare, outline*). Second, they need to write down the important points they want to include. Third, they should arrange the points in a logical order. Numbering each item in priority order can be helpful. Fourth, they need to compose their response. A strategy that incorporates these four steps, suggested by Scruggs and Mastropieri (1992), is referred to as the SNOW strategy. SNOW is an acronym:

S—Study the question.

N—Note important points.

O—Organize the information.

W—Write directly to the point of the question.

Students should also be taught to leave some time to proofread their responses to make sure their answers are complete. In addition, they will want to make sure their handwriting is legible, as well as to check for clarity of response, spelling, and grammar.

- When students are unsure of an answer, encourage them to stay with their first choice and only to change an answer if they are sure it is incorrect.
- Most tests do not have a built-in penalty for guessing. If students do not answer a question, they have no chance of getting it correct. Teach students to make their best guess rather than leaving an item blank.

Bottom Line

✓ Throughout their lives, students will have to take a wide variety of tests. Teachers will help students succeed in school by helping reduce student test anxiety, as well as by providing strategy instruction for succeeding on the different types of test items.

5

Collaborating With Others

Foster Positive Relationships

Knowing how to communicate well is the mark of the true teaching professional and can transform a merely competent teacher into a great one.

—Cheri Cerra and Ruth Jacoby (2005, p. 17)

One of the most important ways to succeed in teaching and in life is to foster positive relationships with others. Your school community consists of a diverse group of professionals, including teachers, administrators, administrative assistants, paraprofessionals, custodians, the school nurse and counselor, and security personnel, as well as students and parents (Thompson, 2007). Also, when it comes to success and high performance at work, research shows that IQ only accounts for about 4–25 percent of success (Goleman, 1998). Goleman suggests that emotional intelligence is a much bigger predictor of success and achievement in work and life than cognitive abilities. *Emotional intelligence* is the capacity to recognize your feelings and those of others, to motivate yourself, and to manage your emotions well, and those that occur in relationships. To be successful, you not only need the knowledge and skills to teach well, you also need the skills to relate well and to build positive relationships with others.

Communicate Well With Others

Good communication skills are the backbone of relationship building. When you initiate and participate in conversations with members of the school community, communication becomes a dynamic exchange of information, thoughts, feelings, and ideas. During the interchange, shared meaning is created, as each person simultaneously conveys and receives information in a reciprocal manner through both verbal and nonverbal channels.

You communicate in direct ways through the content of what you say, as well as indirectly through posture, tone of voice, gestures, and facial expressions. You also have a unique frame of reference and perspective that you bring to relationships based on your past experiences, your temperament, and your attitude and beliefs, which all impact the way you receive and interpret what you hear. If you find yourself making assumptions about what was said based on your own frame of reference, you are likely to miss the intended meaning of the speaker's message. In addition, the person with whom you are communicating has a unique perspective. Whenever you share information, listeners are creating a story in their minds based on their own frames of reference. Without clarification, the potential for misunderstanding is high. Clear, open communication utilizing the skills of rapport building; listening with empathy; and asking clarifying, open-ended questions is useful in building positive connections and minimizing misunderstandings. Below are critical communication skills for fostering positive relationships with others.

Attend to Others and Build Rapport

According to Mehrabian (1980), only 7 percent of communicated meaning is determined by the content and words that are spoken, 38 percent by the tone of your voice and sounds you make, and 55 percent through body language and facial expressions. Strive to deliver a clear message by using verbal and nonverbal cues in addition to expressing the content of your message.

When talking with others, use good attending behavior. Make friendly eye contact with the person you are speaking. Maintain an open, relaxed, and confident posture (e.g., avoid crossed arms, fidgeting, and looking around). Establish an appropriate distance between yourself and the person with whom you are speaking (approximately 3–5 feet when standing). Adjust your communication, the way you carry yourself, and your tone of voice appropriate to the circumstances and the people with whom you're communicating. For example, the way you choose to talk with students at an afterschool club will be different than the way you choose to communicate with parents or your colleagues. If unsure of the relationship and goals of the interaction, it's best to consider your fallback position, which is to err on the side of professionalism. Also, after you ask a question, be patient and wait for the person to respond before asking another question. Encourage conversation by letting people know in small ways that you are listening by nodding your head; leaning forward; and using expressions of encouragement, such as "yeah," "I hear you," "is that so," "uh-hum," "that's nice," and "really."

Listen With Empathy

It has been reported that the average person can speak approximately 150 words per minute, while our inner dialogue occurs at a rate of 450 to 650 words per minute (Tracy, 1993). As a result, it's not uncommon to think about other things when you are listening to someone and/or to be thinking about your reply. You can improve your listening skills by purposefully listening for understanding. Show that you genuinely care about people by striving to be an empathic listener. By listening with empathy, you are listening to both the content of what a person is saying and for the feelings and needs underlying the content. Empathy is the ability to understand the world respectfully from another person's perspective or experience. Listening at this level enables you to pick up on the partially spoken and/or unspoken feelings and needs of another person. It involves the ability to sense and to respond to what other people feel. Reflecting your understanding of another person's experience with empathy is one of the most powerful ways to help someone feel heard and understood. For example, you could respond to a parent's statement by saying, "You sound worried and concerned about your child's performance in reading, and you would really like to identify specific ways to help your son improve his reading skills," or, "You sound really proud that your child is excelling in math, and you're concerned that she may not be challenged by some of the assignments. It sounds like it would be helpful to explore ways to advance your daughter's skills through enrichment activities." When you listen fully to the content of what the speaker has said (i.e., information, facts, and opinions) and for the emotions the speaker is communicating (i.e., feeling words, body language, tone of voice), you are more likely to capture the intended meaning of the message.

The more you are in touch with and able to identify and express your own feelings, the better you will be at recognizing emotions in others. When you express your feelings, strive to follow the statement "I feel . . . ," with an emotion rather than a thought or belief. Four ways to increase your awareness and your understanding of feelings and ability to respond with empathy have been described by Nadler (2007):

1. Listen for feeling words when people are speaking. Feeling words will often stand out in a sentence when someone is talking. For example, "I'm really *disappointed* with the turnout for the open house."

2. Observe gestures and facial expressions. You will notice that people will frequently show their emotions rather than describe how they feel.

3. Reflect your observation through a question such as "You seem quiet today. Is anything bothering you?"

4. Step into someone else's shoes. Imagine how you would feel if you were in his or her situation.

When listening with empathy, reveal your understanding of what was said by reflecting back in your own words the feeling and needs underlying the content of what was said. This gives you the opportunity to verify and clarify your understanding of what you heard. If you notice that your attention has shifted from the speaker to your own thoughts or distractions, shift your attention back to the speaker. If you missed something, you can let the speaker know in a respectful way by stating, "I missed part of what you just said. Could you repeat that?" It's important to note that respectfully listening to and understanding another person's perspective does not necessarily mean you agree with the person. The goal is to practice one of the habits of highly successful people described by Covey (1989/2004): "Seek first to understand, then to be understood" (p. 235). Finally, be sure to avoid major barriers to effective communication, such as judging, arguing, ignoring, interrupting, diminishing, or trying to talk other people out of what they are feeling. Eliminate distractions so you can give the speaker your full attention by turning off your cell phone, setting aside your mail or paperwork, and resisting the temptation to multitask.

Be Curious and Ask Open-Ended Questions

Ask appropriate open-ended questions and open yourself up to the ideas of others. Open-ended questions invite others to share more information with you, while closed-ended questions lead to short yes or no answers. Examples of open-ended questions include "**Tell** me about your day," "**Describe** the project you are working on," "**How** can I be of assistance to you?" "**What's** so important about implementing this plan by Friday?" and "Can you **give** me an example?" Listen with empathy, then reply with an appropriate response and/or ask another question.

Manage Your Emotions Well

At some point in your life, you have probably experienced what it's like to be on the receiving end of someone else's angry outburst, so you are aware of the damage this can do to relationships. When impulsive feelings override rational thoughts, it's possible to say or do things that you later regret, such as yelling, criticizing, or name-calling. Goleman (1998) calls the impulsive expression of strong emotions the "amygdala hijack." The amygdala stores all of your emotional memories from positive to disturbing, and it uses these memories to determine if you are in danger or are at risk. The amygdala scans your experiences for threats by "matching what's happening now with stored templates from the past" (Goleman, p. 75). Although there may be times when you are aware that a memory is influencing your emotional reaction, at other times you are not aware that your current reaction to a situation is even slightly based on past experiences. When a situation poses real danger, the body's fight, flight, or freeze response can be useful in protecting us. However, when you are communicating with colleagues, parents, and students, reacting when you are emotionally flooded can lead to ineffective, disrespectful, or hurtful interactions.

When you are emotionally triggered in response to current events, the amygdala sounds an alarm in your body releasing fight, flight, or freeze stress hormones, including cortisol. These stress hormones increase your heart rate and blood pressure and prepare the muscles in your body to react. High cortisol levels are associated with a decrease in your ability to perform well, remember, and process information (Fralich, 2007). In addition, once these hormones are released, they linger in your body, creating the conditions for the effects of stressful events to compound. Cumulative stress can make you more vulnerable to an emotional hijacking. Threats to self-esteem, such as being treated rudely, perceived unfair criticism, or a loss in job status, can trigger the alarm. Once you are emotionally flooded, pausing before you respond gives the brain's prefrontal lobes the opportunity to mediate this reaction by providing the amygdala with information, such as judgment, reason, and rules, to help analyze your perceptions and to reassure the amygdala that you are not in danger.

Staying calm in the face of stress is based on how well you can recognize and label your own feelings when they are occurring and regulate your own emotion. Practicing good self-care to keep your stress level in check, taking a time out before responding so you can cool off and calm down, and recognizing that you can choose the way you express your feelings will help you maintain composure. For more ideas on how to manage your emotions, see the section in Chapter 1 titled "Maintain Perspective" and in Chapter 6 titled "Balance Your Personal and Professional Life."

Honor Cultural Differences

Your cultural identity and unique perspective affects your ability to understand someone from a different cultural background. It's important to be aware that prejudice and stereotypes are emotional reactions that are learned in childhood. As you get older, you form beliefs that support these views. Even though you strive to be open-minded and nonjudgmental, it's important to be aware that biases from early learning experiences may persist and contribute to your attitudes and emotional reactions when interacting with people from diverse cultural backgrounds (Goleman, 1995). When working with students, parents, and colleagues from diverse cultural backgrounds, it's essential to consider that culture significantly influences the development of an individual's values, beliefs, and behaviors (Friend & Cook, 2007). People who belong to different cultural and ethnic groups share similar norms for expressing emotions and communicating verbally and nonverbally; conversely, diversity can exist among people who share a similar culture. Increase your awareness and understanding of cultural differences by learning specific information about other cultures, strengthening your capacity to be open and embrace diversity. For additional ideas about working with families who are culturally diverse see the section in Chapter 2 titled "Value Cultural and Linguistic Diversity."

Avoid Gossip

Although friends and colleagues may find gossip entertaining, it's essential to remember that gossiping is unprofessional. If you choose to participate in gossip, it will undermine your ability to form open, trusting relationships with members of your school community. People will be reluctant to open up to you if they know you spread rumors or talk about them when they are not present. Set a standard for yourself not to participate in gossip. If someone approaches you with gossip, you can respond in the following ways:

- Ignore the gossip and change the topic. For example, you could say, "I would like to know how you are doing."
- Set a boundary and state, "I'm not comfortable having a conversation about someone when they are not present."
- If gossip is occurring in a group setting, politely excuse yourself and leave the conversation.

Maintain Confidentiality

Familiarize yourself with your school's confidentiality policy. You have access to students' confidential academic records, as well as to personal information about students and their families. You can be held legally liable for disclosing privileged information without a signed release from a student's parent(s). The exception to this is if you suspect the student may be a danger to him- or herself or to others or if you suspect a student is being abused or neglected. In such cases, you are required to report your concerns to the proper authorities. Be sure to follow your school's policies and procedures for reporting suspected abuse or neglect.

Tips for Fostering Positive Relationships in Your School Community

- Maintain professionalism. The way you dress, carry yourself, and keep your classroom as well as the manners and attitude you convey when interacting with others reflect on your professionalism and influence the way others see you.
- Be honest about who you are. Tell the truth, resist the temptation to misrepresent yourself to bolster your status in other peoples' eyes, and respond in ways that are consistent with your values.
- Smile and be friendly. Familiarize yourself with your school community by obtaining a copy of the faculty and staff roster, including any specialists, such as the speech and language or reading specialist, who could be a resource to you. Strive to learn the names of your coworkers.
- Consistently greet people using their name when you can and make eye contact with them at the start of each day. Be the first person to say "Hello" and ask, "How are you today?" If you see them later in the day, give them a smile of acknowledgment.

- Familiarize yourself with your school's policies and procedures for notifying the principal or administration about concerns. Inform the principal when incidents with parents or students' misbehavior could become problematic. Take responsibility and admit your role when you have made a mistake.
- Acknowledge, give credit, and thank your colleagues and the school staff for the work they do.
- Build trustworthiness by keeping your commitments. Follow through with the things you agree to do.
- Be respectful and polite when you make requests and listen to other people's opinions without interrupting.
- Obtain permission prior to borrowing supplies and/or materials from colleagues and staff and return borrowed items promptly.
- Manage chance outside of school meetings with parents and members of your school community gracefully. Be polite and friendly. However, if a parent or colleague wants to talk with you about a student or a concern, encourage the person to call you to set up a meeting.
- Apologize when you make a mistake or hurt someone's feelings. A simple apology, such as "Please forgive me. I'm sorry for _____," can help restore good will.
- Schedule a face-to-face meeting with your coworkers when addressing sensitive issues or resolving conflict rather than using e-mail. Remember, e-mail is a one-way form of communication. Consequently, the potential for the receiver of an e-mail message to misinterpret statements about sensitive issues is greater than in a face-to-face meeting, when you can use your voice and body language to convey your concern in a positive manner.

Bottom Line

✓ The members of your school community want to be heard, understood, and accepted. The ability to foster positive relationships with others is essential for succeeding in teaching and life.

✓ You have the ability to improve your communication skills and to respond constructively in a variety of situations with others. Make a conscious effort to be an effective communicator.

Be a Great Team Player

We don't accomplish anything in this world alone . . . and whatever happens is the result of the whole tapestry of one's life and all the weavings of individual threads from one to another that creates something.

—Sandra Day O'Connor,
Supreme Court Justice (retired)

As an educational team member, collaboration and teamwork are an essential part of your role. One of the primary ways other members of your school community will get to know you is through team meetings. Inevitably, you will be invited to participate in a team activity, be it a coteaching arrangement; a curriculum or professional development team; or a special education team established to assess, determine eligibility, and address the needs of students. You will also participate in faculty meetings. It's important to think about how you want your colleagues and other members of the educational team to know you. Who do you want to be? Do you want to be viewed as someone who is adaptable and collaborative or inflexible and uncooperative? Friendly and agreeable or argumentative and demanding? It is in the context of meetings that your colleagues will form their initial opinions of you, be they favorable or unfavorable.

According to Nadler (2007), during meetings your colleagues will receive "snapshots" of your behavior, your posture, attitude, and interpersonal style. Over a period of a few meetings, including formal or chance meetings in the hall and the teacher's lounge, behaviors that are repeated can be viewed as "who you are." Even though these snapshots don't fully represent who you are, they can become fixed impressions in the minds of others. Positive fixed impressions will help you, in that if you make a mistake later on, people are more willing to make allowances for it. However, if their fixed impressions are negative, it can be very difficult to change them. It is important to be mindful of the way you participate and present yourself in meetings and in chance encounters with your colleagues, administrators, and school staff. Take steps to maintain professionalism and strive to work well with everyone. Be willing to let others get to know you and the contributions you can make to the school community.

Apart from meetings, you can create other opportunities for your colleagues to get to know you by joining them for lunch or by stopping by their classroom to say hello. Demonstrate that you are willing to assume additional duties, such as joining an afterschool committee or helping out with a school club. Show you care about your school community by demonstrating a willingness to collaborate and assist others. However, be careful not to overextend yourself or to allow participation in volunteer activities to interfere with developing your classroom management and teaching skills.

Effective Teams

According to Senge (2000), "schools are rife with teams" (p. 73), including curriculum teams, staff development teams, service development and delivery teams, and administrative teams. Teaming with others to assess needs, develop and deliver services, make decisions, and collaborate on projects can lead to better outcomes (Friend & Cook, 2007). In addition, research has consistently shown that the collective intelligence of the team is greater than the intelligence of individual members (Goleman, 1998). Teamwork can solve complex problems and lead to the accomplishment of great goals. Given the significance of teamwork in schools, it is unfortunate that not all teams function well. At some point in your career, you may have participated on a team that experienced problems or attended team meetings that felt like a waste of time. When team members work together successfully and run effective meetings, the investment of time and energy can be very rewarding. As a contributing member of a team, you are one of a group of individuals with unique skills and perspectives who will put aside self-interest to work together to achieve shared goals. Whether you are participating on a team or leading a team, below are tips and strategies, adapted from Harrington-Makin (1994), for increasing the team's effectiveness:

- The team members have a clear, shared sense of purpose or mission, and the goals and outcomes for which the team is striving are understood by all members.
- The members of the team understand their roles and the importance of their participation on the team, as well as the role of others, and the responsibility for achieving team goals is shared.
- Group processes and shared norms (e.g., behavioral expectations, such as arriving on time, resolving conflict, and consensus decision making) are established and are continually improved.

- The development of trust, social harmony, and risk taking are nurtured and encouraged.
- Leadership is shared, and the open expression of diverse opinions and ideas is encouraged. Conflict is viewed as an opportunity to explore new ideas and to find common ground.
- The team meetings help hold the individual members accountable for their contribution toward the attainment of team goals.

It's important to be aware that high-functioning teamwork does not happen automatically. When a group of professionals join a team to work together for the purpose of accomplishing common goals, it takes time for the team to develop into a high-functioning unit. Teams go through five stages of development (Tuckman & Jensen, 1977):

Stage 1: *Forming*—Team members are polite and cautious as they explore their boundaries and the purpose for working together.

Stage 2: *Storming*—As team members become more comfortable with each other, conflict can arise as the members negotiate and resolve issues pertaining to purpose, procedures, and leadership.

Stage 3: *Norming*—Trust is built as team members reconcile differences, establish ground rules for functioning, and create a shared team identity.

Stage 4: *Performing*—During this stage, the team's efforts are focused on accomplishing team goals.

Stage 5: *Adjourning*—Team members deal with changes in relationships as the work of the team is completed.

Your effectiveness as a team member is demonstrated in your ability to add value to the team by addressing issues, building trust, demonstrating leadership skills, and bringing out the best thinking and attitude of all team members (Lafasto & Larson, 2001). When participating on teams and attending meetings, you can increase your effectiveness in the following ways:

- Keep your commitment to the team by attending all meetings. If for any reason you cannot attend, notify the meeting leader.
- Be prepared and arrive on time.
- Be willing to participate by concisely sharing relevant ideas, opinions, and recommendations.

- Be accountable for the tasks you agree to do and complete them on time.
- Use effective communication skills. Show interest by being attentive. Listen with an open mind, summarize what was said, and ask relevant clarifying questions.
- Being willing to serve a role, such as facilitator, scribe, or timekeeper.

Organize Effective Meetings

Below are suggestions to consider before, during, and after meetings to make them effective and meaningful (adapted from Friend & Cook, 2007).

Prior to the Meeting

- Establish the purpose of the meeting.
- Identify the participants.
- Locate and reserve a meeting room, as well as the equipment and materials needed.
- Send an agenda to the participants that includes the meeting purpose, time frame, location, and topics to be covered along with any materials and premeeting work required. Invite people to notify you of any additional items they would like to add to the agenda prior to the meeting.
- Prepare the meeting room.
- To optimize team functioning, assign key roles to members. Some of these roles will rotate among team members from meeting to meeting. Sample roles include the following:
  a. *Leader*—This person keeps things running smoothly. The leader fosters a collaborative climate and helps the team clarify its goals and stay focused on them. Often the leader calls the meeting and may take care of premeeting tasks and logistics.
  b. *Facilitator*—This person keeps the meeting focused on agenda items. He or she gives everyone the opportunity to speak and helps the team adhere to group ground rules.
  c. *Timekeeper*—This person monitors time spent on agenda items and keeps the team informed of time constraints.
  d. *Scribe*—The scribe documents key decisions, action items, completion dates, and who is responsible. A copy of the minutes is typically distributed to team members within 48 hours.

During the Meeting

- Start the meeting on time.
- Welcome and introduce participants.
- Review assigned roles.
- Review the agenda, prioritize items, and allocate time for each item.
- Summarize and make sure responsibilities and action steps are clear, as well as time lines for completion.
- End the meeting on time.
- Ask for feedback with questions like "What went well?" "What can we change or improve?"

After the Meeting

- Clean up and reorganize the meeting room.
- Make sure the meeting minutes are sent to the members.
- Evaluate the effectiveness of the meeting and consider changes for the next meeting.
- Follow through with assigned tasks.

Bottom Line

✓ High-functioning teams can accomplish great things.

✓ You have the potential to be a valuable team player and to make a powerful contribution to your school community by developing your skills as an effective team member and leader.

Look for Mentors

You've got to ask. Asking is, in my opinion, the world's most powerful and neglected secret to success and happiness.

—Percy Ross (1916–2001),
American entrepreneur and philanthropist

When you arrive at school the first day, you will be expected to perform the same tasks as a 20-year veteran teacher. Fortunately, you will enter the doors of the school with training, enthusiasm, and new ideas. Even so, teaching is intellectually and emotionally complex. It takes experience and time to automatize routines, to develop an array of teaching skills, and to establish strategies that promote students' learning. Therefore, to enhance your professional development, it may be advantageous to identify a colleague to whom you can talk about teaching and other work-related issues. Unfortunately, all too often, new teachers are hesitant to talk about problems or to ask for help because they don't want to appear incompetent.

You may find that your school district has a practice of assigning a mentor, advisor, or helping teacher to work with new teachers. Most often, assigned mentors are experienced teachers who are recognized for their effective teaching and their willingness to help others. They are a wonderful resource! Regrettably, many of these relationships only last for the first year of teaching, and many don't even last that long because both individuals are not committed to the relationship. Consequently, it is in your best interest to take a proactive approach to finding a mentor who will help you develop the attitude, knowledge, and skills to become a master teacher.

If your school district does not assign a mentor, the best way to find a mentor is to look for someone with whom you feel a connection and whom you respect. Once you've identified a potential mentor or two, start spending time with that person. It is best to proceed slowly and let the relationship grow naturally. As you become comfortable with each other, discuss the possibility of formalizing the relationship in a way that will help you reach your professional potential.

Mentors can assist in a variety of ways. Certainly, you want to work with someone who listens, asks questions, identifies resources, and helps solve problems. More specifically though, Lipton, Wellman, and Humbard (2003) suggest that the role of a mentor is to balance three functions:

1. Offering support
   a. Emotional
   b. Instructional (e.g., time management tips, instructional strategies, management routines, assessment strategies, lesson planning and resources)
   c. Institutional (e.g., staff evaluation procedures, resource acquisition procedures, and school duties)
2. Creating challenge
   a. Facilitating reflection
   b. Problem solving and goal setting
   c. Analyzing student performance data

3. Facilitating a professional vision
    a. Setting high expectations for students
    b. Engaging in lifelong learning focused on continuous improvement

To benefit from having a mentor, you will need to overcome your fears of taking a risk and appearing incompetent by asking for help. You will need to commit yourself to the mentoring relationship by meeting regularly, communicating effectively, and accepting responsibility for your own growth and development.

Undoubtedly, many issues you will talk about with your mentor will arise out of daily necessity. You can also use the following questions to stimulate self-reflection and discussion with your mentor:

- What gives you the greatest sense of job satisfaction?
- What do you regard as your major strengths?
- What area would you like to focus on for improvement?
- What aspect of work do you find most frustrating?
- What knowledge would you like to acquire?
- What skills would you like to acquire?
- What experiences would you like to have?
- What helps you most in your work?
- What hinders you from achieving your goals?
- How would you like to be supported at work?

Once you feel established, you also may want to consider serving as a mentor for another colleague. Doing so will provide you with opportunities to develop close relationships with fellow educators, observe different styles of teaching, and influence the quality of education that all students receive.

Bottom Line

✓ Most successful people make the time to seek out guidance and advice from experts in their field.

✓ Lack of time is one of the challenges of working with a mentor. In addition to your regular planned times for meeting, consider eating lunch together, sharing rides to and from school, using e-mail, or calling each other at a designated time.

Partner With Parents and Guardians

Parents are allies; they want what's best for their child and are willing to work with you toward that goal.

—Scott Mandel (2007, p. 3)

When working with parents, it's essential to remember that parents love their child. They believe in their child's potential, and they want their child to succeed in school. As a result, parents are essential partners in the education of their child.

Meaningfully involving parents in their child's education is one of the biggest predictors of success in school. The way you communicate with and engage parents plays an essential role in nurturing and facilitating this partnership. Involving parents in their child's education and maintaining strong home-school communication will create more opportunities for parents to participate in their child's education at home and at school. Involved parents are more likely to communicate with their child about his or her academic progress and/or concerns. According to Mandel (2007), increasing parental communication with children about school is one of the most important factors in enhancing the academic achievement of children.

The Challenge of Family Involvement

Although the importance of family participation in a child's academic development has been well documented, families face challenges that can inhibit parental participation. Among them are economic difficulties that affect access to transportation and child care, conflicting work schedules, fatigue from juggling the multiple demands of family life, different cultural expectations, limited English-speaking skills, and mistrust or disempowerment resulting from poor past experiences working with teachers (Pugach & Johnson, 2002; Turnbull & Turnbull, 2001). In addition, families are diverse and face many unique challenges. Below is a summary of the many factors influencing family life (Federal Interagency Forum on Child and Family Statistics, 2007):

- 20 percent of children speak a language other than English at home.
- 67 percent of children ages 0–17 live with two married parents; 23 percent of children live with only mothers, 5 percent live with only fathers, and 5 percent live with other adults.

Following are additional findings:

- 17.9 percent of families with children under 18 live in poverty (U.S. Census Bureau, 2006).
- Dual-earning couples with school-age children outnumber families with a male breadwinner and female homemaker by three to one (Zimmerman et al., 2001).
- 36.9 percent of women are unmarried at the time they give birth to a child (Martin et al., 2007). Many of these women are in cohabitating relationships, including with different-sex and same-sex partners.
- Many children are living in divorced and remarried families. The divorce rate in America has fluctuated; estimates range from 36 to 50 percent for first marriages, approximately 60 percent for second marriages, and 70 percent for third marriages (Divorcerate.org, n.d.).

Given the diversity of family structure, ethnicity, culture, and economics, it's essential to be respectful and embrace these differences. In other words, be careful not to judge others based on ethnic stereotypes or socioeconomic status or to make assumptions that parents are apathetic or indifferent when other factors may be affecting their involvement. When working with families with limited English-language skills or who are deaf or hard of hearing, arrange to have an interpreter or translator available. Parents need to know that their feelings and concerns are heard and understood so as to trust you. It's important that you do not allow a language barrier to get in the way. Also, when you anticipate limited English-language skills, particularly with immigrant families, consider providing these parents with information in their native language. Several translation resources are listed in Resources at the back of this book.

When children's parents are divorced or remarried, involve the significant adults who will help the child succeed. Include both biological parents and stepparents in the conference. It is optimal for all primary caregivers to have access to the same information, to contribute information, and to express concerns. However, if the relationship between divorced spouses is not conducive to their meeting together, hold separate meetings.

Be Accessible and Maintain Communication With Parents

Give parents ways to contact you. Give them your work e-mail, school address, and school phone number. Let them know when you will respond (within 24–48 hours). Remember that many single parents and dual-earning couples may have difficulty obtaining the time off from work to meet with you or to talk with you by phone. If connecting with a student's parent during normal business hours is problematic, schedule an early morning or early evening phone appointment or face-to-face meeting for these parents. Consider this an investment of time that will help foster a positive partnership with these parents.

Initiate Contact With Parents Early in the School Year

Send parents a positive, inviting message about your classroom philosophy, expectations, rules, events, and homework requirements. Include information about how parents can become involved in the school and ways to support their child at home. Plan to communicate with parents on an ongoing basis. Use a weekly or bimonthly newsletter, e-mail bulletin, or notes sent home to keep parents informed of upcoming events, unit and curriculum changes, and ways they can help. Consider using multiple methods of communication to ensure that you reach all parents. A back-to-school open house is also a good time to meet parents and to provide them with introductory information about the classroom and ways they can contact you. In addition, let parents know you're interested in connecting with them by calling them within the first few weeks of school. You can initiate a positive relationship with parents by giving them opportunities to ask questions and to clarify any concerns they have. Show you are genuinely interested by inviting parents to share any information that would be helpful for you to know about their family and their child.

Make Phone Contact With Parents

- Introduce yourself and let them know you are excited about the opportunity to teach their child.
- Let them know that you believe in building a strong parent-teacher partnership around helping their child succeed in school. Since parents are the experts on their child, explore their ideas about what will help their child succeed in school. Allow them to advocate for their child's needs. Ask if they have any information that would be helpful for you to know about their child (e.g., special needs, interests, strengths, academic challenges, strategies that have helped their child in the past, or challenges with which the family is dealing that could impact

their child). Consider anything that they share about the child's family life as a gift to you. If a parent reveals information indicating that the family or a family member is experiencing financial, marital, or mental health problems, offer to provide community-based referral resources that can assist the family with these concerns and gently redirect the conversation back to the needs of the child.

- Invite parents to think about how they may want to be involved. Let them know (1) ways in which they can volunteer and that you will be following up with a sign-up sheet for help with projects that are planned during the year; (2) how you will maintain communication with them throughout the year (e.g., periodic phone calls, classroom newsletters, meetings; (3) how they can contact you; and (4) when you anticipate the first teacher-parent conference will be.

Keep Parents Informed of Their Child's Progress

Let parents know when their child is succeeding, as well as when he or she is struggling. Communicate any concerns you have about a significant increase in behavioral problems, change in motivation, or decline in academic performance. Create a schedule for sharing grades with parents. If your school provides the option for parents and students to track grades online, update your grade book weekly. For parents and students who do not have a computer or Internet access, periodically send home a grade sheet that parents sign and the student returns to you. It's important not to wait for student-parent-teacher conferences if a child is struggling with academic and/or behavioral difficulties. If it becomes apparent that a meeting with parents would be helpful to address ongoing issues, then initiate it (see information in the next section, "Facilitate Effective Student-Teacher-Parent Conferences," for strategies to work as a solution-focused team).

Promote Parental Involvement

Research indicates that student achievement can be predicted by how well families encourage learning at home; communicate high, reasonable academic and career expectations to their child; and participate in their child's education at school and in the home (National PTA, 1998). Although statistics indicate that 70 percent of parents help their children with homework a minimum of once per week (U.S.

Department of Education Institute of Education Sciences, 2007), it's important to note that the way in which parents become involved also enhances or hinders a child's achievement. Pomerantz, Moorman, and Litwack, (2007) identify four important factors that influence the quality of parental involvement:

1. *Autonomy support*—Children whose parents use a positive approach that nurtures the children's autonomy by supporting them in solving their own problems and exploring their environment fare better in achievement than children of parents whose approach is controlling. Controlling parents tend to pressure their children to do homework and to perform well in school by using demands and commands and/or withholding expressions of love.

2. *Focus on process*—When parents use a process focus rather than a person focus, they praise their children for their efforts and the process of mastering skills. A person-focused approach puts the focus of praise on a child's intelligence, achievements, and innate abilities. Parents whose approach is process focused help develop mastery motivation in their children; *mastery motivation* has been defined as a "psychological force that stimulates an individual to attempt independently, in a focused and persistent manner, to solve a problem or master a skill or task" (Morgan, Harmon, & Maslin-Cole, 1990, p. 319).

3. *Positive affect*—When parents express positive emotions, such as love, caring, and enjoyment in their children's schoolwork, they encourage their children to develop more positive feelings about their work, which can enhance their children's internal motivation. In contrast, a parent's expression of negative emotion, such as hostility, irritability, and criticism of schoolwork, will trigger stress in their children, which can interfere with learning.

4. *Positive beliefs*—When parents communicate that they believe their children are capable of doing well in school, they tend to view their children's academic setbacks as resulting from a lack of effort rather than from a lack of ability. They are more likely to communicate to their children that they think them capable. Children whose parents believe in them develop more self-motivation and are willing to persist when facing academic challenges.

Given the importance of the quality of parental involvement, consider offering an evening parent workshop on how to most effectively help their children with homework. Topics you may want to consider include: classroom homework expectations, how to effectively and affectively help with homework, the importance of routines, and how to help their children get organized.

Bottom Line

✓ Children are in school 15–20 percent of their waking hours (Mandel, 2007). The remainder of the time, they are under the supervision of parents and guardians. As a result, parents have the potential to be powerful partners in helping their children succeed in school.

✓ The way you communicate and work to nurture your relationships with the parents of students will have a significant influence on the quality of this partnership.

Facilitate Effective Student-Parent-Teacher Conferences

Parents have become so convinced that educators know what is best for their children that they forget that they themselves are really the experts.

—Marian Wright Edelman,
American children's rights activist and
founder of the Children's Defense Fund

One of the most important meetings you will facilitate throughout the year is the student-parent-teacher conference. Three of the most important outcomes of the family-teacher conference are to (1) partner with parents around helping their child succeed in school; (2) facilitate the exchange of information about the student's academic progress, academic and personal strengths, behavioral observations, and areas for improvement; and (3) work as a student-parent-teacher team in addressing concerns, setting goals, and solving problems.

Encouraging students to take an active role in participating in evaluating and sharing their academic work during conferences with their parents or guardians has numerous benefits. Among the benefits identified by Borba and Olvera (2001) are the following:

- Parents are more likely to attend conferences if their child is involved.
- Communication between students and their parents increases through the sharing of the students' achievements and academic progress.
- Students who may worry when parents meet privately with their teacher experience less anxiety when they participate in the conference.
- Through self-reflection and evaluation, students take more responsibility for their learning and set goals for their improvement.
- If academic challenges or problem behaviors (e.g., truancy, underachievement, missed homework assignments, rude and/or disrespectful behavior) are identified, students and parents can work together with your assistance to establish a plan of action for addressing concerns.

If parents request to talk with you privately, you can invite them to do so by scheduling a follow-up meeting or a phone conversation. Below is a description of the steps you can take before, during, and after the conference to maximize success.

Before the Conference

Take steps to ensure that all parents are notified of the importance of attending the conference. Inform parents about the conference through your classroom newsletter, a flyer, and/or by e-mail. You also can have your students create and deliver an invitation to their parents or guardians to attend their conference along with a sign-up sheet that gives parents options to pick a time they can attend. Students can assume responsibility for returning the sign-up sheet to you. Confirm the meeting day and time with parents through a return note, e-mail message, or follow-up phone call. Be sure to use multiple mediums for contacting parents.

Prepare yourself for conferences by decluttering your classroom. Involve the students you teach in selecting the work of which they are most proud for their portfolios to share with their parents. Organize progress reports detailing each student's grades and any assessment scores that can help parents understand how their son or daughter is performing in school. It is important to demonstrate to parents that you understand their child's strengths and areas for improvement in each subject area. If parents have not visited your classroom prior to the conference, plan to meet the parents at the office and accompany them to the classroom. Consider planning each conference to last approximately 20–25 minutes. The first 5–10 minutes of the conference can be student led; the second 10–15 minutes, you can join the family and answer questions, reinforce positive academic progress and achievement, facilitate goal setting, and address any problem areas that need attention.

During the Conference

Create an inviting, collaborative environment. Make sure there is appropriate seating at tables for parents to meet with their child. Have students share portfolios of their work. Students can identify and share their strengths, areas in which they feel successful, and areas for improvement. Students can talk with their parents about setting goals they want to work on for the next grading period. Once you join the meeting, be sure to sit with the family and to use active listening to attend to and to respond to parents' concerns in a positive manner. If you need to give parents information about their son or daughter's behavior or academic difficulties, see the next section, "Manage Difficult Conversations."

When setting goals for improvement and addressing problem areas, strive to work together with the parents and student as a solution-focused team. Invite parents to share any information that can help you better understand their child. If you anticipate that you will not have enough time during the conference to address concerns adequately, schedule a follow-up meeting. Consider inviting other multidisciplinary team members to attend the follow-up meeting if it would be beneficial to the student and his or her family.

Work Together to Solve Problems

By working with students and families from a solution-focused approach, you can help family members identify patterns of behavior and individual and family strengths that can be utilized to address a specific problem. The goal is to change ineffective behaviors by identifying and supporting problem-solving behaviors that work. Key assumptions underlying this approach were developed by de Shazer and colleagues (1988, 1991) as a model of brief therapy. These assumptions and questions will assist in (a) developing a clear picture of what an effective solution can be; (b) identifying times when even part of the solution is already occurring; (c) identifying small steps that can be taken to change perspective, feelings, and behavior to reach the desired goal; and (d) obtaining a commitment to do something that will make a positive difference (Durrant, 1995). Below are four key assumptions and questions developed by de Shazer (1988, 1991), Selekman (1993), and Durrant (1995) that you can use to facilitate a solution-focused conversation around a problem behavior:

1. *Change is constantly occurring*—Human life and behavior are constantly changing. As children grow and develop, change is inevitable. Families are also changing. When family members leave home, change jobs, alter the hours they work, or become ill, change affects everyone in the family system. As a teacher, you have the ability to convey the belief and expectation that positive change is possible. Selekman (1993) notes that it is more helpful to think of and to communicate an expectation of when change *will* occur instead of *if* change will occur. Consequently, you want to assume that families and family members have the strengths and resources to change.

2. *Small changes can lead to bigger changes*—Goals can be broken down into small steps that make a positive difference. Small changes in our routines, such as going to bed a half hour earlier, getting organized for the next day the night before, or planning what we will have for lunch the next day, are examples of small changes that can make the morning routine flow more smoothly. In addition, small changes in one family member's behavior can influence change in other patterns of interaction around a problem area.

3. *If it works, don't fix it*—There are always exceptions to problematic patterns. In other words, no problem happens all the time. There are times when the problem does not occur or times when things are going better. A child may be rude and disrespectful to the homeroom teacher yet very respectful to the science teacher. A child may be performing well and turning in homework in reading but have excessive missed assignments in math. A child who "steals other students' belongings" may be honest and respectful of other people's property at times. You can ask about times when the problem isn't occurring and find out more about what goes on when the child is cooperative, turns in homework on time, or is respectful of other people's property. Exceptions provide clues to what the child and family can do more often. The goal is to clarify what's different when the problem is not occurring and to do more of it. For example, if the problem is not consistently completing homework in math, ask, "What's different about the times when homework is getting done?" "What

does the student do?" "What are mom and/or dad doing?" What does the teacher do? "How could you make that happen more often?" Identifying specific behaviors—such as sitting in a quiet place; doing homework at a certain time of day; receiving assistance from mom, dad, or a tutor; or having a parent close by doing paper-work—can all be helpful clues to a solution that could work for this student and family.

4. *If it's not working, do something different*—Sometimes we behave and react to a problem in ineffective habitual ways. It's not uncommon for parents or teachers to become caught in a cycle of trying to solve a problem in the same way and obtaining the same poor results. They may also find themselves trying to solve a problem with the same solution but with more effort. When this occurs, the attempted solution can trigger and/or maintain the problem. For example, a parent's reminding a child to do homework can escalate into nagging and yelling after the child refuses to comply. The child yells back and becomes upset and then gets sent to his or her room, and homework does not get done. When problems have persisted and patterns of interaction around the problem have been repeated, it's possible for family members and teachers to feel stuck and to lose sight of the strengths and resources they have. They can develop a "problem-dominated" view of themselves and look for evidence that supports this view (Durrant, 1995). The "miracle question" and scaling questions—see below—can help students and family members move from feeling stuck to unstuck by opening up possibilities for change, as well as for identifying resources and strengths they already have.

The miracle question was originally developed by de Shazer (1988) to assist people in describing what the future without the problem looks like. An example of the miracle question is "Let's imagine that tonight while you are sleeping, a miracle happens, and the problem is solved. When you wake up the next day, how will you know the miracle occurred?" The inquiry can probe more deeply: "What will be different at home? And at school? What will you be doing differently? Who in the family will notice that you have done that? Are there times when even part of the miracle happens now? What's different about those times?"

Scaling questions are also useful in building on the assumption of change in a positive direction. For example, a question you could ask is "On a scale of 1 to 10 with 1 being really bad and 10 being really good, how would you rate how you are doing now?" You could further ask, "When you are able to say that you have moved up the scale (use a number 1 or 2 points closer to a 10 from the number stated by the student or parent), what will you be doing differently? How will we know you have moved from a 4 to a 6 on the scale?" Strive to obtain a rich description of what moving up the scale looks like. Use the student's and family member's responses to these questions to explore a different approach to solving the problem. For example, parents can be encouraged to do something different. If dad's been in charge of homework, perhaps mom could take over. Or perhaps the parent(s) and the child can change the location or time homework is done. Instead of nagging about doing homework, parents can watch for and make positive comments when their child initiates doing homework and/or works independently. You can check to make sure the student wrote down the assignment, establish a place where the homework gets turned in, and/or provide a special homework folder in which homework is returned to school.

At times, a student or a family member responds to the miracle question or scaling question with an "I don't know," or "I have no idea," response. If you hear such a response, consider asking a hypothetical question to facilitate further dialogue about solutions, such as "If you did know, what would you say?" or "If you did have an idea, what would it be?"

As part of closing the conference, obtain a written agreement of the small steps that will be taken to resolve the problem. Use carbonless paper or make a copy so that the student and parent(s) can take a copy with them. If for any reason during the conference, a parent becomes angry, inappropriate, and raises his or her voice because of dissatisfaction with grades or denied services, or if a parent disagrees with something you have said or done, stay calm and remember that you have the right to ask the parent to stop yelling and to speak calmly. If the parent does not comply with your request, state that the conference is over and that you will ask the principal to contact the parent within the next day or two to schedule another meeting to address his or her concerns (Kelley, 2003).

After the Conference

Thank everyone for attending. If appropriate and time permits, encourage students to show their parents around the classroom. Document any decisions that were made and follow up on any agreed-upon referrals or tasks. Be sure to reinforce any positive changes you see occurring in a student's performance based on the solutions agreed upon in a previous meeting. Send a note home to parents letting them know how their son or daughter is doing. If it becomes clear that a student and family could benefit from the support of a family counselor to help implement and maintain change, consider giving the family the names of three licensed marriage and family therapists in your community.

Bottom Line

✓ The student-parent-teacher conference is one of the most important opportunities you have to build a strong partnership with parents around helping their children succeed in school.

✓ Involving students in evaluating and sharing their academic progress with their parents will increase the likelihood that parents will attend the conference and will help their children take more responsibility for their academic success.

Manage Difficult Conversations

Every human being, of whatever origin, of whatever station, deserves respect. We must each respect others even as we respect ourselves.

—Ralph Waldo Emerson

Many of your colleagues—and perhaps you—were drawn to the teaching profession largely for the love of working with kids, only to find that your career requires you to be a team player, collaborate with others, and work well with a variety of adults, be they colleagues, parents, administrators, staff, paraprofessionals, or community members. The dynamics of relationships, the challenges of communicating well, and the requirement to at times deliver sensitive information to parents set the stage for you to encounter some degree of conflict during your career. Conflicts develop when people interact in response to perceived incompatible differences of opinion, goals, or methods or threats to their resources, status, values, or needs (Friend & Cook, 2007). Although conflict can stimulate a positive search for new information, creative ideas, and solutions, the way conflict is handled can be destructive to relationships. Shoring up your skills in this area will help you work effectively with all members of your school community. Below is a description of essential skills for managing many types of conflict with coworkers.

Manage Conflict Constructively With Coworkers

Begin by assessing if the issue is worth pursuing. If you find yourself experiencing a strong emotional reaction in response to this issue, it's better to wait until you feel calmer to evaluate your feelings and to decide how you would like to address it. Take the time to identify what the issue means to you and what your needs are. Decide how important this issue is to you and whether you can influence the situation. If you decide that the issue is not worth an investment of your time and energy, let it go and move on. If after evaluating your feelings and needs, you decide it's best to address the issue, proceed in a constructive manner by initiating a face-to-face meeting with the person with whom you have a difference. Below is a model for resolving concerns (adapted from Brounstein, 2001).

Prior to Addressing the Issue

- Strive to put your best self forward by maintaining a positive perspective and a respectful attitude. If a conversation does not begin well because you present an issue by blaming or criticizing someone else, that person is likely to respond with defensiveness and will not be able to consider your concerns. Remember that you are part of an educational team. Maintaining positive relationships based on mutual respect is essential for working well with others, regardless of whether you like or dislike the person. The key to being respectful is to view your coworker in a collaborative manner, as a partner working with you to resolve the problem rather than as an adversary. Remember, you are ultimately responsible for managing your own emotions.
- Although you disagree with your colleague, you both have equally valid perspectives. Validating someone else's perspective is not the same as agreeing with him or her.
- Strive to find a win/win solution or a mutually satisfying solution on which you both can agree.
- Take the time to establish a plan or agenda for the meeting to help guide the conversation. This will also help you clarify your request of the other party, as well as what you are willing to offer.

When Addressing the Issue

- Invite the person to discuss the issue in private. Be sure to allocate an appropriate amount of time to address the issue. Make a brief statement about the purpose of the meeting and objective of the conversation in positive manner. For example, you could say, "Mary, I initiated this meeting to talk about an issue that is affecting how well we are working together on this project. I know you mean well, and I really appreciate the expertise you bring to this project. My goal for this meeting is to work out our differences and to find solutions that will improve our working relationship and allow us to successfully meet our deadline."

- State the structure for the meeting. "I would like to briefly state the concern that I have, then understand your perspective on this issue. Once we understand each other's perspective, I would like to work with you on exploring solutions and settle on an agreement we both feel we can commit to."

- Next, briefly state the issue by using "*I* statements" to describe your concern and by discussing the actions of the other person in a matter-of-fact way. Be careful not to interpret or evaluate your observations. Use phrases such as "I have noticed . . ." or "I observed . . ." or "I heard . . ." Then state the impact that the problem is having on you using an *I* statement such as "I feel . . ." For example, you might say, "Mary, I have noticed that you have not responded to the last three requests I have made for information about this project. I feel frustrated and concerned that we are not going to be able to meet our deadline, because I do not have the information I need from you to complete my part of the project."

- Actively listen to the other person's response. Seek to understand the other person's position on the issue. Allow the person you are speaking with to share his or her position without interruption and ask clarifying, open-ended questions to help you understand.

- Listen empathically by reflecting back what you heard the person say in your own words and strive to convey the feelings and the needs implied in the message. Strive to summarize what you heard to his or her satisfaction.

- Please note that on some occasions, your best attempt to address an issue will be met with a defensive reaction. Making sure that the other person feels heard and understood before you clarify or add to your position can help diffuse this reaction.

- If needed, offer to clarify your position on the issue without blaming, judging, or discounting the other person's concerns. Ask, "Can I clarify my perspective?" or, "Let me address a concern that you brought up." Then express your position in a respectful, considerate manner.

- Once a mutual understanding is reached, move toward developing a solution. Offer your desired goal and let the other person respond. For example, you might say, "Mary, I would like to suggest as a goal that we improve our communication by responding to each other's requests in a timely way and clarifying a time line for getting information to each other." If the other person wants to change the wording of the goal statement and you agree, be open to accepting it. This step is about establishing a positive common goal on which you can both agree.

- Once you establish a goal, the next step is to generate ideas for reaching it. Can you both be flexible to compromise around this issue, or can a solution based on a new way to look at the issue accommodate both of your needs or perspectives? Generate possible solutions by asking for ideas from the other person, then offering yours.

Closure

- Make an agreement by selecting a solution that meets aspects of both of your needs. Summarize the plan of action to which you are both willing to commit. Who will do what by when? Commit to putting your agreement in writing and send a copy to the other person. Thank your coworker for his or her cooperation and schedule a follow-up meeting to evaluate the effectiveness of the solution.

- If the issue is unsolvable at this time, determine if there is value in taking additional time to process individually the information shared and to meet again to discuss the issue further. If it's clear that outside assistance will be necessary to facilitate a conversation, request a meeting with an administrator, colleague, or mediator. Finally, if there is no room for flexibility in either party's position but it's possible to proceed by respectfully agreeing to disagree, then do so.

Special Considerations When Responding to an Angry Person

On occasion, you may be confronted by someone else's anger. Whether you are responding to an angry parent regarding a student's grade or a colleague who is upset about the rude behavior of a student in your class, once people are emotionally flooded, it can be very difficult to resolve conflict. It is best to strive to prevent an escalation in anger by staying composed and patient, regardless of the emotions expressed by the person with whom you are speaking. Listen with empathy and take steps to calm the person. Below are tips for communicating with an angry person (adapted from Bender, 2005):

1. Stay calm and breathe.

2. If confronted with anger in a public place at school such as a hallway, consider moving to a more private location. However, please note that if you are concerned about your personal safety or believe that anger could escalate if you speak with this person privately, then stay in a public area. If you decide to move, say, "I can see you're upset. Let's move this conversation where we can talk privately and discuss your concerns without interruption."

3. Allow the person to express his or her concern or position on the issue. Say, "Help me understand what you are concerned about." Set aside your own position so you can focus on that of the other person and paraphrase and validate that person's perspective with empathy. Reflect key feeling words and the needs underlying the feelings. Please note that if the angry person is venting by swearing or being verbally abusive, calmly point out what you're experiencing and ask him or her to stop. For example, "Do you realize that you are yelling (or swearing)?" "I ask that you stop yelling so that I can listen to your concerns." If the insulting behavior continues, politely state that you cannot continue the conversation and that you will call or e-mail to schedule a meeting when the issue can be discussed calmly.

4. If after hearing the other person's perspective, you realize that you made a mistake or hurt someone's feelings, offer a sincere apology. If you do not believe you made a mistake, consider offering a more general statement, like "I'm sorry you are upset about _____."

5. If anger has subsided to the point where the conversation can move into problem solving, ask, "How would you like to see this issue addressed?" or, "How can we prevent this from happening again?" If the request is reasonable, thank the person for bringing the issue to your attention and state what you are willing to agree to do. If you cannot accommodate the request as stated, briefly clarify the limitations of what you can do and suggest a compromise.

6. If you are unable to reach an acceptable resolution, politely end the conversation and suggest that you schedule another meeting to discuss the issue and/or meet with a third party.

Delivering Sensitive Information to Parents

Conflicts between schools and parents can damage relationships, be expensive, and create emotional stress for everyone involved. Factors contributing to conflict between parents and teachers, identified by Lake and Billingsly (2000), include the following:

- A discrepancy between parents' and teachers' views of a child or the child's needs, including grades, academic performance, educational placement, behavioral problems, or disciplinary actions
- Insufficient information about issues like the nature of a child's disability, what constitutes appropriate services, or a student's version of an incident that occurred at school
- A miscommunication or misunderstanding that causes parents to perceive themselves or their child to be devalued or unfairly criticized when receiving feedback or sensitive information. In such a situation, feelings of distrust and defensiveness can emerge. In addition, parents who have encountered past negative experiences with schools may have higher levels of sensitivity.

When you help parents feel valued and respected, coupled with creating clear, open channels of communication, misunderstandings can be minimized and conflicts can be resolved more easily. Below are strategies you can use to communicate sensitive information to parents:

- Remember that you are responsible for maintaining a professional stance that is calm and supportive. Imagine yourself in the parents' shoes and consider how you would want to be informed of your child's academic or behavioral problems (Bender, 2005).
- Provide feedback in a private, comfortable setting and allow sufficient time to address concerns.
- Start with something positive. Thank parents for meeting with you. Describe their child's strengths and what you enjoy about working with their child. Then describe the specific academic concerns or behaviors that interfere with their child's learning. Provide information in a concise, jargon-free manner.

- Provide examples of the child's work and behavioral observations, as well as assessment results.
- Seek input and observations of parents. Listen empathically to parents' concerns or worries. Be sensitive to parents' emotional reactions and address any questions they may have.
- Summarize the concerns and work together to find solutions and determine a plan of action. When appropriate, schedule a follow-up meeting.

Bottom Line

✓ The time and effort you invest in communicating well and developing positive relationships with members of the school community will create a foundation for resolving conflicts more easily when they arise.

✓ When managing conflict, strive to bring your best self to the dialogue by managing your emotions well and seeking win/win solutions.

Recruit and Organize Volunteers

Never doubt that a small group of thoughtful, committed citizens can change the world; indeed, it's the only thing that ever has.

—Margaret Mead (1901–1978),
American anthropologist

Parents and members of your school's community can serve as valuable resources for your classroom. They have a variety of talents and skills that they can share to support the education of the students you teach. Working with volunteers provides you with an opportunity to nurture your partnerships with parents and to build relationships with members of the school's community—be it teachers in training, retirees, members of volunteer groups, or the business community.

You can request help directly for specific projects and/or events, or you can explore what volunteers are interested in and are willing to do and match them with your classroom/school's needs. Also, because of the diverse needs of families and the shortage of time that many single parents and dual-earning couples experience, providing different levels of involvement and a variety of options to assist you in school or outside of school can increase participation among parents.

There are three levels of volunteer commitment:

1. *Brief involvement*—Volunteers may commit to assisting with a one-time event, such as a fundraiser or field trip, or be a guest speaker in your class.

2. *Intermittent involvement*—Parents or members of the community may assist with multiple events throughout the year or be willing to assist periodically on an annual basis.

3. *Continuous involvement*—Volunteers are willing to commit to assist you with tasks and classroom activities on a weekly to monthly basis throughout the year.

Organize the Flow and Activities of Volunteers

Invite parents to sign up to volunteer early in the school year. Inform parents of volunteer opportunities during the back-to-school open house, in your classroom newsletter, and during the introductory phone call you make shortly after the school year starts. You can reach out to the school's community by contacting local volunteer groups or teacher-training programs. Please note that due to safety concerns, some schools have developed policies for screening and selecting community volunteers for in-school activities. If your school has such a policy, be sure to follow it.

Once you have a team of volunteers, you are responsible for planning and organizing their efforts. Some teachers limit the number of volunteers in the classroom at any one time. During some instructional times, perhaps you would prefer not to be interrupted. Create an optimal volunteer schedule and have volunteers sign up during those times. If parents want to volunteer at a time that does not work well in your classroom, provide them with other volunteer opportunities in your school, such as assisting in the lunchroom, playground, school library, computer lab, or an administrative office or helping a different teacher. This strategy can also be useful if on any given day you do not need assistance when a volunteer arrives.

Make sure that volunteers know exactly what to do when they come to your class and that they have access to the materials they need to help you. For example, if volunteers are chaperoning a field trip, provide them with a schedule, safety precautions, and behavioral expectations of the students. Many schools have developed volunteer-training programs. If your school doesn't have one, consider teaming up with another teacher to run an orientation meeting. During the orientation meeting, you can clarify expectations and teach volunteers the best ways to assist and to encourage students when tutoring and when helping with classroom assignments. Consider developing a list of guidelines for volunteers to follow to make the volunteer experience flow smoothly. The following are examples of expectations and guidelines, adapted from Shalaway (1998), for fostering a great working relationship with volunteers. Have volunteers review and sign the form, acknowledging that they have reviewed and understand these guidelines.

- Plan and schedule the times you would like to volunteer in advance.
- If you need to cancel or change a volunteer time, please call the school and leave a message. If possible, please give 24 hours' notice. The best number to call is _____.
- You may choose to stop volunteer activities at any time.
- Sign in at the main office when you enter the building and obtain a volunteer badge prior to coming to the classroom.
- Wear neat, casual attire.
- Engage students positively and model polite, respectful communication.
- Being under the influence of drugs or alcohol is prohibited.
- The advocacy of a religious or political affiliation is not allowed.
- If you have preschool-age children, make arrangements for child care prior to volunteering.
- Do not interrupt a lesson unless it's an urgent matter. Instead, wait for an appropriate time to ask for assistance. If you have questions or concerns about something you observe in the classroom, let me know, and we will schedule a private time to discuss your concerns.
- If you observe a child engaging in inappropriate behavior, let me know so that I can manage and address the behavior since it is not appropriate for you to discipline students.
- All information that you learn about students as a result of volunteer activities is confidential. Please do not share confidential information with others.

I understand and accept the volunteer expectations and guidelines.

Volunteer Signature: _____ Date _____

Teacher Signature: _____ Date _____

Specific ideas about how you can involve volunteers in your classroom are described below:

- *Tutoring students*—Volunteers may make a weekly commitment to assist you during school or as part of an afterschool program. Students can be tutored one-on-one or in a small group in a specific subject area, such as reading or math.
- *Quizzing students*—Volunteers help students review and practice material to improve proficiency in spelling or math and to prepare for tests.
- *Providing clerical assistance*—Some volunteers may prefer not to work directly with students. These volunteers can assist you by making photocopies, preparing art materials, creating a bulletin board, or filing. Remember, if you cannot protect a student's confidentiality, do not give a task such as grading papers and filing students' personal and academic information to a volunteer.
- *Preparing snacks and contributing to classroom parties*
- *Serving as a class parent*—This volunteer may provide information to other parents about upcoming classroom events, help with the classroom newsletter, coordinate volunteers, and create a phone tree.
- *Being a guest presenter*—This volunteer shares an area of expertise or teaches a skill to the class.
- *Chaperoning a field trip*
- *Assisting with an afterschool activity or club*—The volunteer might help out with a music, art, or chess club, for instance.

Parents who cannot volunteer during in-school hours due to their work schedules can assist you in the following ways:

- Locating supplemental teaching materials to enrich student learning around a theme, topic, or new unit
- Giving monetary contributions or donating supplies for a project or for general classroom use
- Participating in the decision-making process by joining the PTO or PTA, a parent advisory committee, or a fundraising committee

Community Involvement

Once you familiarize yourself with the types of learning opportunities available in your school's community, you are likely to find a wealth of resources and volunteers that can enrich the education of the students you teach. There are many ways to make connections with your school's community. Among them are the following:

- Students might participate in a service-learning project, such as visiting the elderly or cleaning up a local recreation trail.
- Local businesses might encourage employees to volunteer in an afterschool club or tutoring program or serve as guest lecturers.
- Museums, parks, national monuments, and businesses offer opportunities for field trip experiences.
- You or your school might collaborate with local volunteer organizations or teacher-training programs.
- Through a pet-partner reading program, students can practice reading to qualified service and therapy dogs in your community. For more information, contact the Delta Society at www.deltasociety .org for registered dogs in your area.

Demonstrate Appreciation and Gratitude for the Help You Receive

It is important to thank and express appreciation to volunteers. Give volunteers recognition for their assistance via a personal thank-you from you and from the students in your class. Recognize the efforts of volunteers in your classroom newsletter or consider hosting a classroom party for volunteers.

Bottom Line

✓ It takes families, communities, and schools to educate a child. Parental and community involvement in the education of students is correlated with higher achievement, better behavior, and increased attendance. You have an essential role in building a team of volunteers to assist you in educating the students you teach.

✓ Tap into the talents, skills, and interests of parents and community members.

6

Taking Care of Yourself

Balance Your Personal and Professional Life

True happiness comes from living an authentic life fueled with a sense of purpose and balance.

—Dr. Kathleen A. Hall (2006, p. 3)

You have made an important investment in yourself to launch a rewarding career as an educator. Now, it's essential to take care of your investment and your greatest resource—you! Research indicates that 22 percent of new teachers leave the profession in the first three years, and after five years, the attrition rate increases to 50 percent (Bobek, 2002). Make a commitment that you will not be one of the teachers who burns out in three to five years. You do have the power to create a personally and professionally rewarding and satisfying life.

One way to create a fulfilling life is to seek balance. What does it mean to be balanced? Imagine what it would be like to balance on one foot for 60 seconds. If you have tried this in the past or are willing to try it now, you will notice that your body makes many small adjustments to stay balanced and to keep from falling. You may find yourself taking calming breaths or focusing to stay centered. Like balancing on one foot, juggling the demands of daily life is a dynamic and challenging process. Creating balance in your life is about how well you navigate multiple roles and responsibilities. Every teacher is faced with the challenge of managing multiple roles, be they spouse, partner, parent, teacher, friend, son, daughter, volunteer . . . and the list goes on. In addition, you are in a service profession that places multiple demands on your time, and there is always more you can do to improve your skills, your classroom, your lessons, and your relationships. Balance is about making the adjustments to stay on course and to find satisfaction and contentment in your life while navigating life's daily challenges.

Among the multiple meanings of *balance,* as defined by *Merriam Webster's Collegiate Dictionary* (2006), is "mental and emotional steadiness." In other words, creating a personally and professionally satisfying life is an inside job as well as an external one. It's about staying balanced internally, even when the demands and stressors of teaching and daily life pull you off course. It's also about the choices you make about how you spend your time. On a daily basis, you are faced with an endless series of decisions about how you use the 1,440 minutes in each day. When you allow the decisions about the way you spend time to be driven by circumstances (e.g., e-mail, work commitments, parents, administrators, students, and other peoples' requests), you can end up feeling time crunched, drained, and out of balance. You have the power to choose your priorities and to create the fulfilling lifestyle you dreamed of while preparing for your teaching career.

Making self-care a priority is foundational to creating a high-quality life and to staying balanced in who you are, regardless of your circumstances. According to an Eisenhower National Clearing House Poll of veteran teachers, "taking care of yourself" was picked as one of the most important pieces of advice to share with new teachers (Deutsch, 2003). Below are six essential, time-tested self-care strategies for maintaining optimum health and perspective. If you consistently practice these strategies, you will manage stress well and increase the likelihood of feeling balanced.

Exercise

The benefits of establishing an exercise routine are significant. Regular exercise is associated with maintaining a healthy weight, getting better quality sleep, having increased energy, reducing health risks, and improving self-confidence. Exercise releases positive endorphins, which help reduce stress and enhance your well-being. Thirty to 60 minutes of exercise five to seven days per week has been shown to improve overall quality of health. Pursuing a workout routine that improves your cardiovascular system and strengthens your major muscle groups is optimal. However, if you are short on time and getting a gym membership does not fit into your budget, you can improve your health just by adding more activity to your day. According to the Mayo Clinic's Foundation for Medical Education and Research (2006), people who move throughout the day, including changing postures, fidgeting, tapping their toes, and walking more, stay leaner. Create ways throughout your day to move frequently. Following are a few examples:

- Park at the far end of the parking lot and walk to the entrance of school.
- Spend your lunch break walking with a colleague rather than sitting in the teachers' lounge.
- Walk inside the bank, restaurant, or dry cleaner instead of using the drive through.
- Take your dog for a walk.
- Purchase exercise equipment or exercise to a video workout.
- Play with your kids. Based on the age and abilities of your child, bike, walk, rollerblade, or play an active game together.
- Join a team sport, such as volleyball, tennis, softball, or bowling, to enhance your social network as well as exercise.
- Join a dance, yoga, or Pilates class.

Eat Well

Research has confirmed that your health is significantly affected by what you eat. In many ways, you are what you eat. Eating well can reduce your chances of developing heart disease, obesity, diabetes, or digestive problems and can improve your energy level and overall sense of well-being. Make healthy food choices by planning meals and snacks for the week when preparing to go to the grocery store. When you cook, create "plannedovers"—that is, leftovers that can be frozen and used for lunch or dinner on another day. Limit your intake of coffee, sugar, and junk food. The average adult consumes between 1,600 and 2,000 calories per day, depending on height, weight, and activity level. Eat regular meals to keep your energy up and to avoid overeating at mealtime. Choose snacks that are low in fat, sugar, and salt, such as nuts, dried or fresh fruit, protein or high-fiber bars, veggies and low-cal dip, low-fat muffins, or yogurt. According to the

Mayo Clinic (2006), the recommended number of servings per day for a 1,600-calorie diet are as follows:

- *Three healthy fat servings totaling 135 calories*—For example, a daily serving of fats includes 1 teaspoon of olive oil, 7 almonds or 8 peanuts, and $\frac{1}{6}$ of an avocado.

- *Five servings of proteins or dairy totaling 550 calories*—For example, a daily serving of protein includes $2\frac{1}{2}$ ounces poultry, 1 large egg, 3 ounces of fish, $1\frac{1}{2}$ ounces of lean beef, or $\frac{1}{2}$ cup of legumes.

- *Six carbohydrate servings totaling 420 calories per day*—For example, a daily serving of carbohydrates includes 1 slice of whole-grain bread, $\frac{1}{2}$ bagel, $\frac{1}{2}$ cup of cooked pasta, $\frac{1}{2}$ cup cereal, $\frac{1}{3}$ cup cooked brown rice, and 1 small muffin.
- *Five or more servings of fruit and vegetables totaling 420 calories*—For example, a fruit serving size might be 1 cup of grapes, 2 tablespoons of raisins, 1 medium orange, or 1 small apple. A serving size of vegetables might be 1 cup of sliced broccoli, 1 cup of sliced cucumber, $\frac{1}{2}$ cup of baby carrots, or 2 cups of shredded lettuce.
- *Limit sweets to 75 calories per day.*

Sleep Well

Sleep is a basic necessity of life that is essential for maintaining good health. Despite these findings, many people lack sufficient sleep. The National Sleep Foundation's Sleep in America Poll (2005) found that U.S. adults average 6.9 hours of sleep per night. When time is running short due to personal and professional demands, a good night's sleep is often sacrificed. However, the cost of not prioritizing sleep can be high. Poor quality sleep or insufficient sleep increases your vulnerability to stress and can lead to difficulty with concentration, poor decision making, irritability, fatigue, and, ultimately, a decline in work performance. Although the right amount of sleep varies for each individual, experts on this topic typically recommend 7–9 hours of sleep per night. Here are some tips to ensure you get an optimal night sleep:

- Avoid eating two hours prior to going to bed and avoid food and drinks containing caffeine and refined sugar. Depending on how sensitive you are, you may want to avoid caffeine and sugar after 3:00 PM.

- Create a relaxing evening routine that slows your pace prior to going to sleep.
- Regulate your sleep cycle by going to sleep around the same time each evening and waking up at the same time each morning, regardless of how much sleep you had the night before.
- If you are unable to fall asleep within the first 15 minutes, get up and go to another room. Pursue a quiet activity that will increase the likelihood that you will feel tired (e.g., reading an academic book or an encyclopedia). Then return to bed once you feel sleepy.
- Limit your bedroom activities to sleeping and intimacy. Watching a television show or the news may make it difficult to relax.
- Limit the time you spend in bed to eight hours. It's better to maintain a consistent sleep rhythm than to develop irregular sleep habits.
- If you take an afternoon nap, do not sleep for more than one hour to minimize interference with your ability to fall asleep in the evening.

Breathe Calmly

When under stress or when you experience strong emotions, the muscle tension in your body can contribute to shallow breathing in your upper chest. Shallow breathing can create feelings of tension and anxiety by contributing to irregular breathing patterns, such as breath holding or incomplete exhalations. Research has shown that breathing deeply into your diaphragm or abdominal region can increase your body's relaxation response and reduce your heart rate and blood pressure (Harvard Medical School, 2002). Breathing deeply into your abdomen will facilitate the full exchange of incoming oxygen and outgoing carbon dioxide. Breathing diaphragmatically can help you control muscle tension and reduce stress-related physical sensations of anxiety.

One way to calm yourself and to increase your body's relaxation response is to do a breathing check. Notice how you are breathing right now. Is it centered in the upper part of your chest, or is it in your abdominal region? Is your abdomen gently rising and contracting with each breath? If you find yourself taking shallow breaths, you can learn to breathe more deeply or use deep breathing as a strategy for managing stress. Here is one way to use purposeful breathing as a way to relax:

1. Sit or lie down in a comfortable position. Close your eyes and notice how you are breathing. Place one hand below your rib

cage so that you can feel the rise and fall of your abdomen with each breath.

2. Breathe in slowly and deeply to the count of 4, pause, and exhale to the count of 4. With each exhale, say a relaxing word or phrase to yourself, such as "I am relaxed," "I am calm," or "I feel at peace."

3. Repeat this exercise for three to five breaths.

Once breathing diaphragmatically becomes more natural to you, incorporate this awareness into your daily life. Take a moment throughout your day to take one to three purposeful, calming breaths. For example, try taking one to two calming breaths the next time you are stopped at a traffic light, downloading information on your computer, waiting for a parent or colleague to answer the phone, or sitting at your desk. Over time, you will find that increasing your awareness of your breathing can serve as a centering exercise that helps you become more mindful of the present moment and calms your mind and body. For information on mindfulness and meditation practices go to the Mindful Awareness Research Center (MARC) Web site (www.marc.ucla.edu).

Give Yourself the Gift of Time

You may rarely feel caught up with all the work-related and personal tasks for which you are responsible. It's essential to take time for yourself to pursue activities that give you pleasure, such as listening to music, exercising, reading, relaxing, or doing something fun. As you would schedule an important meeting, schedule blocks of time for yourself during the week. Scheduling nonnegotiable appointments with yourself makes it easier to say no to other peoples' requests for your time.

Seek Support

Having a strong network of supportive relationships is a tremendous buffer for stress and a significant contributor to overall happiness. According to Rath (2006), having a best friend at work can significantly increase job satisfaction. People with three or more close friends at work are 96 percent more likely to report being extremely satisfied with their lives. Seek opportunities to expand your social circle and to deepen the relationships you have. Friends, colleagues, relatives, companions, or a spouse or partner are potentially vital relationships that can nurture you and enhance your life. You can choose to seek support by reaching out to these people rather than managing your challenges alone. When you have had a stressful day or are in need of support, schedule a stress-relieving conversation with a trusted friend or companion. When in doubt about how to handle a situation at school or in your personal life, reach out and ask for help. If you are experiencing a difficult life transition or loss, enlist the support of at least three friends. Tell them specifically what they can do to support you, be it to help with running errands, call you and remind you of your strengths, help you prepare for a challenging meeting, or be available for a supportive phone call.

If you evaluate your support system and find that it could use expanding, consider ways to meet new people. Find out what you can do in your community to volunteer, take a class, or join a book club. Make a commitment to put yourself in situations where you can meet people who share a common interest.

Nurture Your Spirit

Cultivating a sense of purpose and meaning in life and fostering personal growth are essential components of nurturing your spirituality. Research consistently shows that a rich spiritual life is associated with higher levels of physical and emotional well-being. Spirituality can be cultivated in a religious context, as well as through nontraditional approaches, such as meditation, spending time in nature, or developing a connection with something larger than oneself. Many people gain a sense of meaning and purpose from their faith. Religious practices have also been correlated with healthier lifestyle choices, more social support, and a belief that life has meaning by answering some of life's deepest questions (Myers, 2000). A common desire among people who practice all faiths is a desire to develop a connection with the divine power of love and ultimately to learn how to be a more loving human being (Richardson, 1999). Ultimately, love and compassion are part of our true nature (Dalai Lama, 2003). Find ways to nurture your spiritual self on a daily or weekly basis, whether by participating in a religious community, engaging in a private meditation, taking a walk in nature, or engaging in an act of compassion and love.

Overcome Excuses

If after reviewing these strategies, you find yourself thinking, "These are good ideas but . . . I'm just too busy," or ". . . I feel guilty," (which implies you are doing something wrong by taking care of yourself), consider the consequences of not taking good care of yourself. Too often, when people are under stress, they stop doing the things that make them feel better. Someone says to himself, "I'm too busy to go to the health club," so he doesn't exercise. "I don't have time to eat well today," so she snacks on junk food. "I've got to work late," so he doesn't get enough sleep. Then a downward spiral becomes the norm. People become less productive at work, and they have to work longer and harder to keep up. Unfortunately, the cycle can go on until they become overwhelmed, depressed, anxious, or physically ill. Think about what small steps you can take in the next week or month to make some changes. If the needs of others are getting in the way of taking care of yourself, remember the airline oxygen mask demonstration. The demonstration states that you put the mask on yourself first and only then assist your child or others. If you take the time to take care of yourself, you will have increased energy and enthusiasm for taking care of others.

How Do You Know When You Feel Out of Balance?

Review the common distress signals below. Notice how stress affects you personally.

- Irritability
- Feeling overwhelmed
- Decreased concentration
- Feeling helpless
- Trouble falling and/or staying asleep
- Fatigue and emotional exhaustion
- Loss of enthusiasm for work and/or things you used to enjoy
- Decreased performance and an "I don't care" attitude
- Withdrawing from colleagues and friends
- Frequent headaches

If you experience any of these distress signals, do not ignore them. A high level of chronic stress over time is a leading cause of burnout. Increase your self-care. Seek support from trusted family, friends, and coworkers, or if you need assistance in developing and maintaining a course of action, seek the help of a professional counselor or life coach.

Top Ten Ways to Take Care of Yourself at School

Teaching is a demanding profession. Knowing how to take care of yourself at school is essential for maintaining balance and perspective. Strategies for taking care of yourself at school include the following:

- Stay organized, keep your desk uncluttered, and be prepared for the day.
- Post inspirational quotes and favorite pictures in your work area.
- Keep nutritious, high-energy snacks in your desk and plan a healthy lunch for yourself.
- Stay healthy by washing your hands often and keeping tissues and hand sanitizer on your desk.
- Take care of your voice. Straining your voice beyond its natural pitch can lead to voice loss and, over time, could damage your voice. Let the students you teach know that at times, you will use nonverbal cues to prompt them. Examples include clapping your hands, flicking the classroom lights on and off, and counting down (i.e., 5, 4, 3, 2, 1).
- Seek support from colleagues and administrators when you need it. Cultivate a sense of community in your class and recruit volunteers to help you.
- Plan something you can look forward to in the course of every day, such as taking a brisk walk during a break, enjoying a favorite treat after lunch, having a conversation with a colleague, or reading a favorite book to your class.
- Bring humor into your class. Humor will help build rapport with students and foster creative thinking. Lighten things up by keeping a joke book on hand. Tell a joke to your class or play a fun game.
- Stretch with your students or do a mini relaxation exercise with them.
- Do not take a student's or parent's rude behavior personally.
- Review what went well every day. Celebrate successes; learn what you can from mistakes and then let them be.

Take a Moment

Identify three small steps you can take to increase your self-care today. Remember, action steps are specific, measurable, and have a reasonable time frame. See the section later in this chapter titled "Achieve Your Goals" for additional information.

Action steps: _____

_____

_____

_____

_____

_____

What support do you need to ensure the actions are taken? _____

_____

_____

_____

_____

_____

Whom can you count on to support you in achieving your goals? _____

_____

_____

_____

_____

_____

Make Peace With Your Inner Critic

Life shrinks or expands in proportion to one's courage.

—Anaïs Nin (1903–1977),
Cuban-French author

Successful teachers convey a sense of confidence in their knowledge and in their ability to teach. By being enthusiastic, speaking clearly, answering questions with assurance, being decisive, and admitting when you don't know the answer or when you have made a mistake, you demonstrate the qualities of a successful, confident teacher.

According to Nadler (2007), self-confidence is a distinguishing characteristic between average and high-performing professionals. Self-confidence is knowing and believing in your abilities.

You engage in an inner dialogue with yourself every waking moment of your life. What you say to yourself on a daily basis affects what you believe and how you feel about yourself and influences the choices and actions you take. All new teachers experience some level of fear and vulnerability when starting out due to concerns about how well they will perform in the eyes of students, school administrators, and parents. The voice of the inner critic consists of internalized negative judgments about yourself that reinforce your fears and self-limiting beliefs that prevent you from making changes and taking risks. Unfortunately, the inner critic can be self-sabotaging by underestimating your abilities and by preventing you from participating in experiences that challenge you and help you grow. In other words, the inner critic can steal your confidence and courage. The critic can tell you things like "You're not ready to do that," "You're not good enough," "You're not qualified," and "You'll sound stupid." Your inner critic can also overly focus on what you could have done better (Richardson, 2002).

If you only listen to your self-doubting inner critic, your perceptions of yourself and your abilities will be inaccurate. This, in turn, will impact the choices you make and your behavior. Because of past life experiences, some people have a more negative, louder inner critic than others. The good news is that you can make peace with the inner critic by not accepting its false messages and evaluation of you as fact. Instead, view the voice of the inner critic as just one opinion. It's important not to try to control the inner critic; rather, observe what it has to say. Fighting with the inner critic will only increase the time you spend thinking about the self-limiting thoughts. Instead, just observe the inner critic's comments and redirect your attention to developing a more positive internal voice based on an honest evaluation of yourself. One way to do this is to pay attention to your self-talk. Are the messages you give yourself critical or positive? Are you asking yourself questions that lead to a critical answer or a positive answer? Questions like "What's wrong with me?" "How could I mess this up?" and "How stupid could I be?" only encourage you to identify evidence from past and present situations to form critical statements about yourself.

To make peace with the inner critic, it's essential to ask yourself the kind of questions that will lead to an honest, positive dialogue with yourself, which builds confidence and guides you toward constructive action. The next time your inner critic is presenting you with loud negative self-statements, stop, breathe, and reflect on the five questions below to help you choose an alternative response that builds your confidence:

1. If a close friend or someone I loved knew I was saying this to myself, what would he or she tell me?

2. What experiences have I had or evidence do I have that shows me that the inner critic is underestimating my abilities?

3. What strengths of mine or positives in this situation am I overlooking?

4. Based on a fair and honest dialogue with myself, what can I learn from this?

5. What response can I choose now that best serves my health and positive sense of self?

Bottom Line

✓ Remember that the messages you give yourself will have a significant influence on how you feel about yourself, the choices you make, and your behavior. Don't shortchange yourself by only listening to the inner critic. Energize yourself and build your confidence through an honest appraisal of your strengths and abilities.

✓ You have the power to choose to be your own best friend and to advocate positively for yourself when you take risks, make mistakes, and stretch yourself to try new things.

Love Your Personal Life and Your Career

It's time to start living the life you've imagined.

—Henry James (1843–1916),
American and British author

Many teachers are drawn to the profession not only for the love of teaching and working with kids but also for the lifestyle teaching affords, only to find that the demands of the profession spill over into their personal life. Grading papers and preparing for classes, teacher-parent conferences, meetings, and extracurricular activities frequently require time outside of school hours. Research indicates that on average, teachers spend 1 hour, 45 minutes working beyond the hours stipulated in their contract each work day (Drago, 2007). Although it's important to develop your skills and do the work necessary to succeed and to experience mastery in your career, it is also important not to become so identified with your professional role that you neglect your personal life or postpone making time for the people and activities that will enrich your life outside of school. If you find yourself thinking that a work-centered life is essential for paying the bills and buying the things that will make you happy, it's time to change your perspective. Research indicates that once basic needs are met, then regardless of age, race, and socioeconomic status, having more money and material possessions adds little to personal happiness (Baker & Greenberg, 2007). You have the ability to manage intentionally the responsibilities of teaching in a way that allows you to maintain quality time for the people and activities that are most important to you.

Be mindful of how you choose to spend your time outside of work. Are you engaging in activities that reflect your priorities and enhance the quality of your life, or are you coming home from work, sitting on the sofa in front of the TV, and eating takeout food or TV dinners out of fatigue and habit rather than for enjoyment? Are you allowing work to intrude into your personal life to the point where you are neglecting important relationships or feeling disconnected from the people you love and care about? Personal fulfillment occurs when you live in congruence with your personal beliefs about what you value most. Values are core principles that reflect who you are and represent what you believe to be of worth in your life. Ultimately, you have the ability to live a rich, meaningful life in which the choices you make and the actions you take are aligned with your core values.

Take a moment and reflect on what you will do to make your life more fulfilling. Are you living your life in congruence with what you value most? Write down your top five values at this stage of your life (see the next section, "Achieve Your Goals," for a sample list of values). Your values and intentions are like a compass that can help guide you in making choices about how you spend your time when life invariably bounces you off course.

My top five values at this stage of my life are

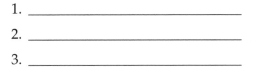

1. _____

2. _____

3. _____

4. _____

5. _____

Now, imagine what it would be like to spend your time in a way that reflects what's most important to you. Responding to the following questions is an invitation to explore your level of satisfaction with various areas of your life. Below are questions for reflection to consider in light of your values. Take the time to write your responses to these questions in a journal so you can review and/or revise them later.

- When you are 90 years old and reflect on your life, what do you want to say about your life and your priorities?
- What do you dream about being, doing, and having in your life?
- In what ways do you make time to connect with the people you care about and love?
- What activities do you enjoy outside of work that enrich your life (e.g., volunteer work, hobbies, cultural events)?
- In what ways do you nurture your personal and/or spiritual growth (e.g., participating in educational activities; engaging in religious or other spiritual practices, such as meditation)?
- What do you enjoy doing for fun and recreation (e.g., spending time with family or friends, taking a vacation, planning a work-free day for yourself, attending a social event, taking personal time for a walk in the woods, or reading a great novel)?
- How do you take care of yourself on a daily and weekly basis (see the first section in this chapter, "Balance Your Personal and Professional Life," for self-care strategies)?
- In what ways do you manage and maintain your financial health?
- What areas of your life are underdeveloped and need more attention?
- In what areas do you feel overextended?
- What are you willing to let go of to make time and space for your priorities?

Now, notice the areas in your life where you feel satisfied that your actions are consistent with your values and those that you would like to give more attention. What are you willing to commit to changing to live in congruence with your values? Identify three changes you are willing to make (see the "Achieve Your Goals" section to develop a plan for implementing these changes).

1. _____

2. _____

3. _____

Make Time for Your Priorities

Freeing up time for your priorities may require setting limits on how much time you spend working or engaged in activities that do not fit with your priorities. When you're at school, choose to be focused and productive; when you're home or engaging in leisure activities, enjoy them. Make a conscious decision not to allow preoccupation with work to steal time from the things that are important to you outside of work. One way to set limits on work is by making the choice not to bring work home. Consider staying after school for 30 to 60 minutes, or if you're a morning person, go to school early to finish grading and prepare for the day. If that is not possible on any given day, compartmentalize your time by designating a block of time as personal or family time. For example, from 5:00 to 8:00 PM, turn off the cell phone and e-mail and save grading and planning for later. You can also set limits on the amount of time you spend on a task. If you plan to grade from 8:00 to 9:00 PM, be focused and accomplish what you can do in an hour. Then set the task aside for another time. The key is to remember that your career can bring meaning and purpose to your life, but your life is not your career.

Work and Family Life

Many dual-earning couples and single-parent families successfully navigate the challenges of balancing work and family life. Below are strategies for prioritizing time for your family by cultivating rituals for connection.

Most parents believe that having close family bonds is an essential factor in a child's development. However, due to the hectic pace of life, many families lack time for fun, recreation, and good conversation. Consequently, many conversations between parents and their children are about the things that need to be done and how they are going to get done. Although discussing logistics helps keep daily routines running smoothly, it does little to nurture relationships among family members.

If you have experienced a shortage of time in your family life, make a commitment to look for ways to structure more time together.

One way to create structure is to build rituals for connection (Doherty & Carlson, 2002). Create family rituals, such as game night, movie night, a parent/child date, or bedtime story time and chat. Also, prioritize time for family meals. According to Doherty and Carlson (2002), eating dinner together is associated with many positive outcomes for children and adolescents, including better nutrition, academic success, and a decrease in risk for substance abuse and early sexual behavior. Use mealtimes as opportunities to be together and visit. Don't eat in front of the television or answer the phone during meals. Make spending time together the priority. If your schedules don't permit you to eat dinner at a regular time, consider having a snack early and eating together as a family later. Eating out as a family is also an option. Planning unstructured time together on the weekends will increase the likelihood of connection, even if it's just part of a day, such as a morning, afternoon, or evening.

If you have a significant other, research has shown that couples who spend a minimum of five hours together during the week have more satisfying relationships (Gottman & Silver, 1999). Establish a daily or weekly ritual for nurturing your relationship. This may include visiting after dinner or when the kids are in bed, planning a weekly date night, going for a walk, or meeting for lunch. When you spend time together, make nurturing your friendship a priority by updating your knowledge about who your partner is and how he or she may be changing over time. Ask open-ended questions to encourage conversation about what's important in each other's lives, such as work, family life, current priorities, dreams, goals, challenges, and desires. Identify small ways you can demonstrate to your partner that you love him or her on a daily basis by expressing appreciation and engaging in acts of kindness and love.

Cultivate a Culture of Teamwork in Your Family

Many couples successfully negotiate and share household responsibilities, such as cleaning, grocery shopping, meal preparation, laundry, monitoring homework, bedtime routines, transporting kids, scheduling appointments, and decision making. If your home responsibilities are overwhelming, discuss what you can afford to hire out, such as to a cleaning service, laundry service, lawn service, grocery delivery service, or child care assistance or by ordering prepared meals. Involve your children in assuming responsibility for chores based on their ages and abilities. Consider holding a family business meeting and use a family calendar to share responsibility for tracking social commitments, family obligations, and significant events. Plan ahead to avoid schedule conflicts and to anticipate where more help may be needed. Also, identify ways and times to have fun as a family and write them on the calendar (Haddock & Zimmerman, 2001).

Bottom Line

✓ Success in finding the right balance between spending time nurturing and taking care of what's most important to you and attending to the needs of the students you teach involves personal assessment, planning, and structure.

✓ Limiting how much work you bring home, sharing responsibilities for managing and running a household with family members, using outside resources, and structuring time to connect with the people you love will support you in creating an optimal balance between work and family life.

Achieve Your Goals

Goals are dreams with deadlines.

—Dr. Diana Scharf-Hunt,
time management author

Do you ever daydream about

- vacationing on a beautiful beach and reading an engrossing book during spring break?
- applying for a grant to participate in a summer institute in Ireland?
- running a half-marathon?
- writing an article for a professional journal?
- visiting Australia?
- becoming the school's literacy specialist?
- learning to play the piano?
- volunteering one evening a week for a homeless shelter?

Do any of these activities interest you? What goals do you have for yourself?

The daily demands of school and home often leave little time to think about the future. Unfortunately, if you don't know what you want to achieve in life, opportunities for growth are likely to pass unrecognized, and you may end up feeling unfocused and unfulfilled.

Each of us has within us an untapped reservoir of dreams and desires. However, too often we race through our lives without pausing to consider who we are, what we want to do, or where we want to be 5, 10, or 20 years from now. Regrettably, no matter who you are, you only have 168 hours to live each week. Given the hours required for work, sleep, and maintenance, it is critical that we use our precious time to create a rewarding professional and personal life.

On a daily basis, you experience the positive results that planning has on teaching effective lessons or facilitating successful meetings. In a similar manner, making time to plan can positively shape your life by providing the focus and clarity you need to attain your goals.

To reach your goals, you need to be able to identify what you want, why you want it, and how you are going to achieve it. One of the first steps in establishing your goals is to create a vision of what you want. Your vision is a general statement that bridges the gap between where you are now in your life and where you want to be. Goals provide the specific, tangible, time-limited steps you will take to actualize your vision.

Values

Goals based on what you really value are more likely to inspire internal commitment and motivation. When you fail to achieve your goals or feel unfulfilled once you reach a goal, you may have set the wrong goal. If you chase goals that are media inspired or are based on pleasing others, you are likely to lose steam or feel discontent. Your values can provide the answer to the question "Why is the accomplishment of this goal important?" Living a life that conflicts with your values can lead to distress. For example, valuing security but living beyond your means or valuing time with your family but having little time left after teaching all day, coaching basketball, and commuting leads to feelings of dissatisfaction. Neglecting your core values is a formula for a stressful, unfulfilling life.

Clarifying your values can provide you with a tremendous source of energy. Ask yourself, "What values are important to me at this stage of my life? What do I deeply care about?" Staying focused on your values at this stage of goal setting, rather than focusing on things to do or have, will help you understand what you're passionate about in life. Identify three values on which you want to focus over the next six months. Examples of values include the following:

Achievement	Fun
Adventure	Growth
Autonomy	Happiness
Balance	Health
Being debt-free	Independence
Challenge	Integrity
Community	Love
Compassion	Making a contribution
Confidence	Security
Creativity	Service
Exercise	Spending time with the kids
Family	Spirituality
Freedom	Travel
Friendship	Wealth

Vision

Now that you have identified your values, begin asking yourself questions that will help clarify your vision: "What do I want and why do I want it?" "How does this fit with what is most important to me?" "What does it look like?" "What does it feel like?" "What will I be doing differently"? Be specific. If you find yourself thinking "I don't know what I want," ask yourself: "If I did know, what would I say?"

Goals

What transforms a vision into reality is the willingness to formulate goals and to take action. Once you have identified your top three values and your vision for what those areas of your life optimally look like, the next step is to turn your vision into specific goals. A goal is a statement about how you will achieve your vision. For example, if your vision is to be healthy, you could set the following goals: to take a multivitamin daily; to reduce caffeine intake to two cups of coffee per day; and to exercise for 30 minutes per day, four times per week.

Goals are effective if they meet the SMART test (Carter-Scott, 2000). Identify the goals for each of the values on which you have decided to focus. Critique each goal using the following five criteria:

Specific—Is your goal specific? Does it precisely define what you want?

Measurable—How will you know when the goal is achieved?

Attainable—Is this goal possible for you to achieve given your characteristics, resources, and limitations?

Realistic—Does your goal make sense given your current circumstances?

Time Based—Each goal needs to have a target completion date. Without an attached date, a goal is a stated intention, not a desired outcome. You can always change a deadline if needed. Missing a target date is an opportunity to reevaluate and set another, more realistic date.

One significant obstacle to goal attainment is trying to work on too many goals at the same time. Unfortunately, this can dilute your ability to focus. It's important to prioritize. Select the most important goal and begin to work on it. If you feel you have multiple important areas to work on, limit yourself to a maximum of three goals to optimize your effectiveness. Once you have determined your goal(s), list all the possible things you can do to move forward and make your vision come true. Find one step that resonates with you. Do the first step you selected and then—choose another step and do it. If you work at it, it won't take long to achieve the steps that allow you to accomplish your goal, be it getting an advanced degree, learning to play tennis, or improving a significant relationship.

Structure your environment in a way that optimizes your success. For example, if you are working on improving your health, organize your refrigerator in a way that supports this goal by keeping nutritious, low-fat food choices available. Set up a walking date with a friend four times per week after work. Use your support team by asking for help from people who believe in you; ask them for support on a daily and/or weekly basis. Reserve time to work on your goal by saying no to things that are not truly important to you. Then use this time to work on your goal by building it into your schedule.

Remember that change rarely happens in a straight line. It's often two steps forward and one step back. When setbacks occur, process your emotions, and put the experience in perspective. Rather than beat yourself up with questions like "What's wrong with me?" or "Why can't I do this?" ask, "What's right with me?" "What is the next step I can take?" and "What are my choices now?" Then move forward. Make an effort to celebrate the attainment of each small step of success.

Bottom Line

✓ The process of setting goals provides direction and focus to your life.

✓ Your brain is a goal-seeking organism. You need to provide it with stimuli so that it can work consciously, as well as subconsciously, to achieve your ambitions.

✓ Specific goals produce specific results. In contrast, vague goals produce vague results.

Set and Maintain Boundaries

The price we pay for avoiding "life's difficult conversations" far exceeds the discomfort we feel from having them.

—Margie Warrell (2007, p. 121)

Do you find yourself saying yes to things that you later regret doing? Do you take on other people's problems at the expense of your own needs? Boundaries are a set of limits that you can establish to protect yourself, prevent overscheduling, and ultimately take care of yourself. Examples of setting boundaries in your personal life can include enforcing a limit that you set for your child, asking an ex-girlfriend or boyfriend not to call you, or turning down a request from a friend or family member to borrow money. In your professional life, boundaries can include choosing to leave the teacher's lounge rather than participate in gossip about a coworker or student; choosing not to talk about a subject that you feel is too personal to share with a colleague; or turning down a request for your time, such as a request that you attend a school function or meeting.

Setting clear boundaries will protect you by helping you make choices about who and what you allow into your life and who and what you keep out. Through boundary setting, you will teach others how to treat you. Healthy boundaries may be both rigid and non-negotiable; for example, it is never acceptable to harm you physically. At other times, boundaries may have some flexibility to them, depending on circumstances and with whom you're setting limits.

Learn to Say No

As a teacher, it is essential to be a team player. At times, this means volunteering to take on additional responsibilities or staying late to assist a colleague with a project. However, sometimes respecting your own needs will conflict with requests for your time. If a request for your time does not align itself with what's important to you, providing a decisive answer by saying no up front will save you time.

One way to evaluate if you struggle with setting limits is to observe how often you regret a commitment you make. Developing awareness is the first step. Pay attention to how often you do things that you would rather not do. Initially, it's helpful to challenge yourself to create a gap between a request for your time and your response. Instead of responding automatically, consider saying, "Let me look at my schedule, and I'll get back to you." Once you decide to turn down the request, consider saying, "I'd really like to, but I can't." Or counteroffer by suggesting an alternative or compromise. Make a clear statement without a long explanation (Hewlitt & Hewlitt, 2003). For example, instead of saying yes to a request to get together with a friend on a Tuesday evening, knowing you have a full day of teaching and afterschool commitments on Wednesday and you would rather have personal time in the evening, say no or suggest an alternative, such as a Saturday morning walking visit. You are entitled to express your wants and negotiate a mutually beneficial option.

Boundaries in Professional Relationships

One of the challenges you face is determining how close to allow yourself to become to the parents of the students you teach and to your colleagues. Unlike the medical or counseling profession, the field of education does not have well-articulated boundaries for teacher-parent relationships. In addition, it is not uncommon to experience times and situations where you may feel stuck, taken for granted, or in a lose-lose situation with a colleague or parent. Difficult work relationships can be a tremendous source of stress. When you continually feel frustrated, upset, or angry about someone's behavior or a repetitive situation, this is a good indication that it is time to set a boundary. Below are boundary issues that you may encounter.

Sharing Personal Information

How much personal information do you want to share with your colleagues? Do you prefer to keep the details of your personal life private? How much do you want to know about your colleagues' lives? Sharing too much personal information before you know a colleague as a trusted friend can lead to gossip about you. Developing a close friendship with a colleague can be very rewarding and can enrich the time you spend at school; however, a close friendship tends to develop over time as you learn you can trust that person.

Relationships With Parents

Since there are no set rules about teacher-parent relationships, it's up to you to determine what professional boundaries you want to establish. Issues to consider include these: How available do you want to be? Will you give out your home phone number or personal e-mail address? Would you consider privately tutoring a student from your class if a parent asked you? Would you go out to lunch or attend a dinner at a parent's house if a parent invited you? Boundaries in this area may be flexible within limits, depending on the needs of the families and students with whom you work. Many of the parents of the students you teach may prefer you to be flexible to accommodate their needs. It's appropriate to be flexible within limits. Rather than being on call for parents, unless it is an emergency or urgent issue, require parents to schedule a phone appointment with you at designated times before or after school. Limit calls to 15 minutes. If you decide to communicate with parents via e-mail, create an auto responder message that lets them know you will respond to their message within 24–48 hours.

Workplace Bullying and Harassment

According to the Workplace Bullying and Trauma Institute (2007), 37 percent of U.S. workers have been bullied, and another 12 percent of workers have witnessed it. *Bullying* can be defined as repeated verbal abuse (e.g., humiliation and ridicule, destructive criticism, name-calling), offensive behaviors that are threatening or intimidating, or work interference (e.g., inappropriately blocking promotion and training opportunities, excessive and inappropriate monitoring, denying access to information required to perform work-related responsibilities). In addition, it is not uncommon for people who experience bullying to suffer from stress-related health problems, such as anxiety, panic attacks, and depression. If you believe that you are being bullied at work, there are steps you can take to protect yourself (adapted from Holmes, 2005):

- Document the incidents of bullying, your communications with the bully, and any attempts you have made to address the issue assertively.
- Talk to a trusted friend or family member about the situation to help evaluate whether to take further action.

- Request a copy of your school district's policies against work-place bullying.
- Request someone from administration to mediate a meeting to resolve conflict with the bully.
- Consult with your professional association or teachers union.

Sexual harassment is illegal under Title VII of the Civil Rights Act of 1964.

> Unwelcome sexual advances, requests for sexual favors, and other verbal or physical conduct of a sexual nature constitutes [sic] sexual harassment when submission to or rejection of this conduct explicitly or implicitly affects an individual's employment, unreasonably interferes with an individual's work performance or creates an intimidating, hostile or offensive work environment. (U.S. Equal Opportunity Commission, 2002)

If you are being sexually harassed, you can protect yourself by telling the harasser that the behavior is not welcome and must stop, reviewing your school's and your school district's policies regarding reporting, and filing a complaint and requesting assistance from your district's human resource department.

Boundary Issues at School

Your Classroom and Desk

Although your classroom and desk belong to the school, teaching affords you the opportunity to be creative and to personalize the space. Consider what your expectations are of yourself, your colleagues, and the students you teach when it comes to respecting your personal belongings, school supplies, and classroom. Examples of issues you want to consider are these: How do you feel about a colleague who borrows equipment or materials from your class? How would you react to a colleague who leaves your classroom a mess after he or she uses it? Will you allow students to have access to your desk?

Time

Are you typically on time for meetings, or do you run late? Do you finish projects on time, or do you procrastinate? Your relationship with time will influence how well you tolerate other people's behavior. How do you feel when people arrive late for meetings? In general, being on time is professional and respectful of your commitment to others.

Commitments

Are you prepared for meetings? Do you follow through with commitments that you have made? Whether you choose to keep your agreements or not reflects on your integrity. Only make commitments to people and projects that you plan to keep.

Student Information

It is never appropriate to break student confidentiality outside of school, and it is only appropriate to discuss student concerns with a colleague in light of trying to help a student succeed at school.

When and How to Stand Up for Yourself

If you find yourself repeatedly feeling emotionally charged about someone's behavior or a situation, this is your opportunity to assess whether to set a boundary. If the source of your feelings is a one-time misstep, then depending on the situation, it may be more appropriate to make allowances for a mistake and move on. If it becomes an ongoing issue that upsets you, however, it's time to address it. Whether you are upset by a colleague who repeatedly allows his or her classroom to get loud to the point of disrupting your class, who borrows items from you and does not return them, or who is repeatedly late for meetings, you can use the five-step process (adapted from Crowley & Elster, 2007; Rosenberg, 2003) described below to help you release your anger or frustration and to set a clear boundary.

Step 1: Release.

When an event or someone's behavior triggers a strong emotional response, you may feel emotionally flooded. This can trigger an increase in heart rate and release adrenaline, which can interfere with your ability to think clearly and to evaluate the situation accurately. Managing your internal response first is essential to dealing with a difficult situation or interaction constructively. It's important first to detach yourself physically and emotionally to reduce the strong reaction you feel. Detach by taking a time-out. Very few situations are so urgent that you have to address them immediately. Take time to calm and relax yourself. Practice calm breathing (see the first section in this chapter, "Balance Your Personal and Professional Life"), take a walk, exercise, step outside, or read. In Steps 2 and 3, give yourself time to process your experience privately. Write down your responses.

Step 2: Clarify.

Reflect on what is bothering you. Evaluate the facts by describing what happened. Then describe how you feel about the facts. What is their role in the situation? What is your role? How do you feel about the facts? What do you need? What are your choices?

Step 3: Identify What You Need and Formulate a Request.

The goal is to communicate your request in a manner that resolves problems rather than implies judgment or anger. What do you need or value? What can you say that could bring resolution to the issue? Is there a request you would like to make?

Step 4: Express Your Concern and Make an Assertive Request.

Begin with the facts. Describe your observation without judging or blaming.

When I _____ (observe, hear), [state the feeling] I feel _____ (emotion or sensation), because I need/value _____. [Then make a direct request.] Would you please _____? [or] Could you _____?

Step 5: Follow up.

Use a strategy to document your request, such as an e-mail, memo, or letter, or make it an agenda item for a meeting. There may be times when it's necessary to reinforce a boundary by restating your request.

Bottom Line

✓ You have the ability to define your own boundaries in relationships. Make it a habit to evaluate what's important to you before you agree to a commitment that could add stress to your life.

> ✓ Resist the temptation to let frustration and anger build up in an attempt to avoid conflict. If an issue that upsets you continues to reoccur in your personal or professional life, that is your cue to take action. Unhook yourself emotionally. Then you can evaluate your concern and address the issue, either by setting a boundary or accepting it and letting it be.

Manage Yourself and Your Time

Every moment of time is unique and unrepeatable—a gift that literally comes once in a lifetime.

—David Ellis (2002, p. 159)

Although there are rarely enough hours in a day to accomplish everything you want, there are ways to make the best use of the time you have so that you can make your days flow more smoothly. Managing time well is about prioritizing time for the things that are most important to you. In addition, you can eliminate habits that sabotage and waste valuable time. Three of the biggest time drains to watch out for are procrastination, perfection, and disorganization.

Behaviors That Waste Time

Procrastination

Procrastination, or putting things off to the last minute, can lead to significant stress, pressure, and insufficient time to complete the task well. Although some people perform well under pressure, many people do not. Make a habit of getting each task done during the time scheduled for it in your planner. If you find yourself procrastinating because you do not want to do the task, consider either delegating it to someone else or just making the choice to prioritize it and get it done.

Perfectionism

Perfectionism can also contribute to procrastination. Although perfectionism is a trait that helps people strive to excel, it can also lead to postponing getting things done for fear of failure or not getting things "just right." In addition, perfectionism can waste valuable time by causing people to spend more time than necessary completing certain tasks or setting unrealistic goals. Don't spend unnecessary time on unimportant tasks or chase unattainable goals. Instead, give your most important high-priority tasks your quality time.

Disorganization

Disorganization wastes time. Have you ever spent 20 minutes looking for your car keys or plan book? All of us occasionally experience forgetfulness or a lapse in organization. However, if you find yourself wasting blocks of time looking for the things you need on a regular basis, it's time to take steps to organize yourself so you will have more time. Below are essential strategies for structuring and organizing yourself and your time.

Strategies for Using Time Well

Prioritization

When you are time crunched and overwhelmed, it's hard to decide what's important. Often, you end up responding to urgent but low-priority items and run out of time for the things that are really important. Time management is about making sure that the way you spend your time reflects what's most important to you in the course of a day, week, or year. According to Covey (1989/1994), the key to time management is to prioritize your schedule by identifying and scheduling your priorities.

You can use the ABCs of prioritization (Dittmer, 2006) to determine what's important. *A* items, or high-priority items, are tasks that are essential to the success of your personal and professional life and are either good personal habits and/or have a short deadline. In other words, high-priority items include the things that if you did them consistently in your personal and/or professional life, you would achieve positive results that would move you toward your big-picture goals, such as maintaining optimum health, spending time with the people you love, or pursuing a collaborative project with a colleague. High-priority items are also essential tasks that need to be completed to perform your job well. Stated another way, you could lose your job if you don't take care of them.

B, or medium-priority items, are important to complete, but you have more time to get to them. These items can move into the *A* list as the due date draws closer. And *C,* or low-priority items, are tasks that you would like to get to if you have the time but are just not that important and are not essential to complete. You may periodically review the list of *C* items and consider moving some of them up to the *B* list.

Below is a four-step process adapted from Ellis (1998) for prioritizing your weekly tasks. For optimal time management and planning, consider planning your schedule in two-week increments.

Step 1: Generate a list of tasks to be completed in the next two weeks based on your responsibilities as a teacher, your roles (e.g., spouse, parent, friend), and your values and goals. Consider writing tasks on 3 × 5 inch cards for easy sorting.

Step 2: Sort tasks according to the ABC method of prioritizing, estimate the amount of time you will need to complete each task, and set deadlines for completion.

Step 3: If you find that your *A* tasks require more hours in a week than you want or are able to commit to, instead of overscheduling yourself, evaluate your tasks further. Consider delaying, delegating, or deleting some of these tasks:

Delay it—What tasks could you delay or move to *B* priority? Some tasks have little value and may be better left for later or left undone altogether.

Delegate it—Identify the tasks you can delegate to someone else, be it a student, classroom volunteer, family member, or friend. Or hire out a task by paying someone to help you if you can afford it. At home, this may mean hiring someone to help you with cleaning, household chores, or maintenance. Remember, when you delegate a task, you are still responsible for overseeing that the task is completed properly.

Delete it—Are you keeping something on your to-do list that just isn't worth doing? If so, delete the task altogether.

Step 4: Use a planner and schedule time for your high-priority items over the next two weeks. Leave some blocks of time open for unexpected urgent tasks. Review your list weekly.

Organization

First, clear the clutter. If you haven't used an item in the last two years, it's time to get rid of it. If you can't part with it because you think you might need it, box it up, label it, and put it in storage. This includes clutter in your classroom closet and old files in your file cabinet.

Second, organize your desktop. Create an in-box system that organizes your paperwork and tasks. You can use a file box or filing crate or place hanging files in a wire rack that you keep on or by your desk. Create files for each category, such as grading, to be filed, reading material, correspondence, lesson plans, lesson plan ideas, and the substitute teacher folder. Keep active files with tasks that need attention on your desk. Use your filing cabinet to store other materials.

Time-Saving Tips

- Begin your day the night before by reviewing your schedule and organizing yourself.
- Create a structure for handling routine high-priority tasks. Strive to have your teaching materials ready and activities planned one to two days prior to when you will be teaching the lesson.
- Stay on top of routine clerical tasks by entering your grades in your grade book and on the computer on a daily basis. And file your lesson plans at the end of each day so you can easily find them the next time you need them.
- Keep a book, journal, or grading material with you. Use precious minutes when you are waiting for a meeting to start, an appointment, or standing in line.
- Use a planner to track your schedule and important meetings.
- Create a classroom newsletter to send home weekly or bimonthly communications to families to reduce unnecessary questions.
- Respond to e-mail messages once or twice per day. Use an auto responder message to indicate that you will respond to your messages within 24–48 hours.

Bottom Line

- ✓ Strive to spend most of your time on the *A* items. If you have put your to-do list to the ABC test, spending your time on high-priority items will give you the best return on your time.
- ✓ Once you schedule time to complete a task, make a habit to get it done.

Deal With Paperwork Effectively

Success comes before work only in the dictionary.

—Anonymous

One of the least desirable aspects of teaching is paperwork. Yet like most professionals in other lines of work, you are required to write plans, complete forms, record progress, keep files up-to-date, and write letters and reports. Accordingly, you will need to develop an efficient system for managing these tasks, or they will negatively affect your teaching effectiveness, as well as your personal time.

On a daily basis, you will handle hundreds of papers, including attendance records, students' work, notices, letters, forms, catalogues, and permission slips. The following are suggestions for helping you to reduce the time and effort needed to complete paperwork in a timely manner:

- Establish a specific space, such as a file cabinet drawer, where you keep all forms in separate file folders. Keep the most frequently used forms (e.g., attendance reports, lunch count) in the front of the drawer and the rarely used forms (e.g., field trip permission slips, purchase orders) in the back of the file drawer.

- Keep materials that contain sensitive or confidential information (e.g., completed report cards, medical reports, Individualized Education Programs for students with disabilities) in a drawer that can be locked.

- Develop sample forms and letters that can be stored and saved on a jump drive. You can then insert the specific information into the form or the letter that applies to the particular situation, print it, and send it and, in the process, save yourself lots of time over the course of the school year. Examples of such notes and forms include checkmark or fill-in-the-blank notes to colleagues, responses to parents' notes, letters sending positive news home, classroom incident reports, itineraries for field trips, telephone conversation/e-mail logs, student participation and homework logs, and upcoming events/meetings notes.

- Acquire and use carbonless copy paper. These can be used for handwritten notes to students, families, colleagues, or administrators. The primary advantage is that carbonless copy paper allows you freedom from being near a computer while simultaneously retaining a copy for your files without having to run to the copy machine.

- Create an individual folder for each student. Arrange the folders in alphabetical order in a lockable file cabinet. When you receive a piece of paper about a student, write the date on top and file the paper in the back of the student's folder.

- Establish a designated place for students to submit their seatwork and homework. Grade them, record the grades, and file or return the work to students. Teach students how the system works and demonstrate what you expect them to do with the materials once they have been returned to them.

- Establish a file folder, either a hard copy or an electronic database, of lesson plans, worksheets, study guides, quizzes, and tests into which you consistently place recently used items. Refer back to these folders as references in following years.

- Try to check your mailbox at the beginning of the day, during your planning period, and at the end of the day. When possible, get into the habit of reviewing the material immediately and either (1) throwing it away, (2) acting on it, or (3) filing it; try not to let it pile up.

- Keep your calendar and/or plan book with you when you read memos from administrators. Enter the dates and times of meetings or tasks with deadlines and place the memo in the back of a designated file folder in case you need to refer to it at a later time.

- Create a specific folder for all of your professional paperwork. Examples include your contract, human resources paperwork, teaching license, observations and evaluations, and professional development transcripts. Keep it in the locked file cabinet.

- Take a few minutes daily to file papers. In addition, try not to give tests or have projects due on Fridays, so you don't end up spending the weekend with the need to grade the work hanging over your head.

- Save easy tasks, such a making copies and filing papers, for the times of the day when your energy is consistently at its lowest (e.g., end of the school day).

- When grading papers, planning lessons, and completing reports, try to minimize distractions and interruptions by finding a place to work that is away from students and colleagues.

- You don't have to grade every student assignment. Many assignments are practice activities. To save time and to provide students with timely feedback you can (1) correct students' papers as you circulate around the room while they are completing seatwork, (2) have students exchange papers and check their peers' work while you discuss the answers with the whole class, or (3) let students check their own work against the answers displayed on the overhead or SMART Board.

- Try to make a habit of returning phone calls or responding to e-mail messages during your planning period or lunch break rather than waiting to the end of the day, when you are often mentally and emotionally drained.

Bottom Line

✓ Although completing paperwork is often tedious and time consuming, it is an essential component of your work. Developing and reviewing paperwork helps you make educational decisions about students. In addition, sharing paperwork fosters communication with other professionals and families.

✓ For more than 50 years, teachers have expressed concerns about the amount of paperwork they are required to complete. It is likely that this issue will not disappear in the next 50 years. Develop a system that works for you and use small blocks of time throughout the day and the week to manage the inevitable stress that accompanies completing paperwork.

Develop a Substitute Folder

Even if you are on the right track, you'll get run over if you just sit there.

—Will Rogers (1879–1935), Cherokee-American humorist and social commentator

It is inevitable that you will miss a day or two of school due to illness, personal business, jury duty, or professional development. Since there is no way to know for certain when sickness or emergency will strike, you will want to plan ahead and develop a generic substitute teacher packet that you leave in your top desk drawer where it can be easily found. Include at least two days of plans in the packet. In addition, you will want to find out about your school district's policy and procedures for missing work. Specifically, you want to know whom to contact, the contact's phone number, and when you are required to call.

The Emergency Substitute Teacher Packet for Unplanned Absences

The substitute teacher's folder should contain the following:

- A copy of your schedule, including the times each class begins and ends
- A class roster and seating chart
- A list of the class rules and an explanation of routines
- Procedures for attendance, lunch count, dismissal, and boarding buses
- Attendance sheets

- A map of the school
- A description of what to do in case of a fire or other emergency, including the evacuation route students are expected to follow
- Information about students with special needs (e.g., students who need to go to the nurse at an exact time of day to take medication or a student who has an Individualized Education Program with objectives different from the other students)
- A description of any duty assignments you have (e.g., playground duty, bus duty, hall monitor) and a brief explanation about how to fulfill the responsibility
- The name and room number of a colleague whom the substitute teacher can contact if he or she has specific questions
- Location of supplies, instructional materials, and equipment
- Schedules of paraprofessionals, volunteers, peer tutors, and related service providers
- Examples of free time activities for students who complete their work

Planned Absences

If you start to feel sick and think that there is a possibility that you may not come to school the next day, write out plans for the substitute before you leave school for the day. This action eliminates the worry of waking up to write plans and trying to get the plans to school in time. If you feel better overnight, then you don't need to use the plans. Similarly, you will want to leave detailed lesson plans for the substitute teacher when you are taking a personal day or attending a professional development workshop. The following are additional suggestions for helping the substitute teacher have a successful day and for you to be able to return to school without having to deal with chaos:

- Ask the substitute teacher to write you a short note to let you know what was completed, what went well, and what needs improvement.
- If you know you are going to miss school, prepare students for the substitute teacher by reviewing the rules of the class and by informing them that you expect them to behave appropriately. Use the note from the substitute teacher to provide students with feedback when you return.
- If you plan to leave seatwork for the students to complete, make the copies yourself, label them, and place them with your plans so the substitute teacher can find them easily. Ask the substitute teacher to collect the work students have completed so you can review it when you return. Also, ask the substitute

teacher to inform students when handing out the assignment that the work will be collected and turned in to you to examine.

- Don't expect a substitute teacher to teach an innovative lesson (e.g., a class debate on a controversial subject or a mini lesson on reading comprehension strategies for expository texts). Rather, develop your plans based on what the students you teach can do independently or in small groups.

- Avoid asking substitute teachers to show movies or to take students to the library. When possible, leave review material or enrichment activities related to the topic of study.

- Copy and suggest that the substitute teacher use some of the ideas presented in Chapter 3 titled "Incorporate Activities" in case students complete their work early.

- If the substitute teacher has been effective, let the administration know so he or she will be invited back. Skilled substitute teachers are beneficial for students, and you and your colleagues will feel more at ease knowing that a competent professional is in charge.

Bottom Line

✓ It is likely that you will miss school at some time during the school year. To diminish stress, take the time early in the year to develop an emergency substitute teacher folder. Update it as often as possible.

✓ When you know you are going to miss school, leave detailed plans and leave plenty of work so that the substitute teacher isn't forced to control the students for large blocks of time without them having specific work to complete.

Be a Lifelong Learner

The key to student growth is educator growth.

—Bruce Joyce and
Beverly Showers (1995, p. xv)

The transition from an industrial age to an information age has changed our lives at a faster rate than at any time in recorded human history. In our global world, we have seen incredible advances in medicine, biotechnology, manufacturing, and engineering. Yet along with those gains, we have seen a concomitant requirement for each of us to deal with exponentially increasing amounts of information and to be able to apply it to a wide variety of contexts. No longer will a fixed body of knowledge, once mastered, be useful for life. Instead, knowledge and skills must be updated on a regular basis. Therefore, personal and professional development is considered a standard condition for surviving in our information-based society.

Personal Development

Carl Rogers wrote, "The good life is a process, not a state of being. It is a direction not a destination" (1961, p. 72). The research to date on quality of life suggests that people who report high levels of happiness tend to be (a) involved in close, positive relationships; (b) actively engaged in and committed to their work; and (c) actively striving toward the attainment of goals and perceive themselves as making progress in reaching those goals (Blocher et al., 2001). To avoid getting into ruts or caught up in patterns and habits that are not beneficial, it is critical that you take time to reflect and learn from your past and that you create a living and learning cycle that helps you to produce an upward spiral of growth (Covey, Merrill, & Merrill, 1994). A simple three-step cycle that has applications for teaching students as well as for promoting personal growth, introduced by Hohmann and Weikert (1995), is shown below:

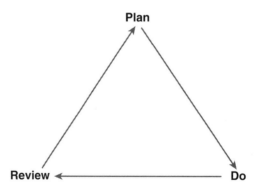

Making time to address each aspect of the model fosters a cycle of learning, which provides the foundation for continuous improvement. As explained by Reutzel and Cooter (2000), "Learning is not the result of development; rather learning is development. Errors are not to be avoided or minimized, but are to be viewed as evidence of seeking to learn" (p. 32). Review, the last step in the process, provides the stimulus for returning to the first step, planning, which begins the process again but with greater insight and capability. When you review, identify what you want to change. Is it an attitude? A behavior? A habit? Acknowledge the obstacles you think you will face if you try to make the change, conduct a cost analysis of making the change, and develop a plan for implementing the change. See the sections earlier in this chapter titled "Balance Your Professional and Personal Life" and "Achieve Your Goals" for additional information related to this topic.

Professional Development

Professional development is a term used to describe the continuing education of educators. Other terms, such as s*taff development, inservice, teacher training*, and *human resource development,* are often used interchangeably. However, some of these terms may have a different meaning for specific groups or individuals. Regardless of the term used to describe the learning opportunity, the objective is to enhance the knowledge and skills of educators so that they can increase student learning (Joyce & Showers, 1995). The following are examples of the different ways that you can be involved in professional development. While each method is presented separately, it is highly possible that you may be involved in several approaches simultaneously.

Conversations About Teaching

As noted in the section in Chapter 5 titled "Look for Mentors," many school districts have established formal support networks through new teacher induction programs. As part of the program, a mentor is assigned to the new teacher to offer assistance and to promote professional development. Mentor programs, when properly implemented, help teachers succeed and feel satisfied (Daresh, 2003).

Whether you participate in a formal mentor program or not, it is beneficial to talk with your colleagues about topics such as school and district procedures; classroom organization and management; connecting with students; assessment, grading, and evaluation; the curriculum; working with families; and the daily stresses of teaching. Be curious about how others do things; be motivated to learn and improve your craft; and be respectful of the knowledge, skills, and experience that your colleagues are willing to share with you.

Individual Professional Development

In addition to interacting with your colleagues about the art and science of teaching, you can pursue your own professional development via a variety of avenues. Educational resources, such as texts, journals, magazines, and the Internet, allow you to choose the information you want to learn about. They also provide you with the convenience of being able to carry them with you so that you can read them during short blocks of time. You also can attend professional meetings and workshops made available by the school district or the state education association.

You may also want to join a professional association. Many national and state organizations exist. The Web site addresses for some of the most well-known professional education organizations are provided in the Resources at the back of this book. Special interest professional organizations exist for almost all subjects (e.g., reading, mathematics, science, geography, history, art, and music), age groups (e.g., preschool, elementary, middle school, and high school), and interest areas (e.g., giftedness, administration, technology, outdoor education, curriculum development, and learning disabilities). Three additional benefits of joining a professional association have to do with the fact that most associations (1) host conferences that provide avenues for interacting with members of the education community, examining and gathering materials, attending practical sessions on topics of interest to you, and listening to effective speakers who are often leaders in their respective fields; (2) produce newsletters and journals and provide communication forums in which members can interact; and (3) provide online computer networks and resources, such as databases, documents, reports, and materials, as well as specialized training opportunities.

Another option is to enroll in an advanced studies program through a college or university. You can take a course or two, pursue a certificate, or seek a graduate degree. Some of the benefits of advanced study include (1) the opportunity to address issues relevant to your daily experiences in the classroom, (2) adding an additional endorsement or license that will make you more marketable, and (3) advancing on the salary scale. Advanced studies courses are also being offered in a variety of formats. Examples include face-to-face courses offered evenings, on weekends, or in the summer; online courses offered over the Internet; and hybrid courses combining some face-to-face classes and some online work.

Group Professional Development

Increasingly, schools have embraced the use of learning communities to address issues (e.g., school improvement plans, increasing family involvement, assessment practices) and to implement curriculum interventions (e.g., literacy, math, bullying prevention). In this approach to professional development, small groups of teachers gather on a regular basis over an extended period to exchange information about a specific topic of study. For example, if the kindergarten and first-grade teachers in a school or school district implement a new reading program, they may attend a training session together for a few days during the summer to become familiar with the intervention, to review the scope and sequence of the curriculum, and to practice teaching and providing each other feedback about the implementation. Then, when the school year begins, the teachers initially meet weekly as a group to discuss the challenges and the successes they have experienced putting the program into action. After that, the teachers divide into pairs and observe each other while teaching and share their observations with each other. Subsequently, the large group convenes again to discuss further their collective observations and to build their knowledge and skills about using the new reading program. The primary benefit of this approach is that you interact with, learn from, support, and think with your colleagues about how to become a better teacher and how to impact positively the learning of the students you teach.

Bottom Line

✓ Leading a personally fulfilling life and becoming an accomplished teacher takes time, reflection, and perseverance. The sophistication of your thinking and the strategies you acquire will be influenced by the quality of the personal and professional experiences you undertake.

✓ The pace of daily living and the structure of the school day make it challenging to take time to reflect and to make changes. Yet reflection is a critical component of the learning process. To develop increased knowledge and a wider repertoire of skills and strategies implementation of the plan-do-review cycle is essential.

Resources

Web Sites

General Resources

Abcteach—http://www.abcteach.com

A to Z Teacher Stuff—http://forums.atozteacherstuff.com

Busy Teachers' WebSite K–12—http://www.ceismc.gatech.edu/busyt/

Carol Gossett's Kindergarten Connection—http://www.kconnect.com

Classroom Connect—http://www.classroom.net

CoolFreebieLinks—http://www.coolfreebielinks.com/Teachers_Freebies/index.html

Discipline Help: You Can Handle Them All—http://www.disciplinehelp.com

Discovery Education Classroom Resources—http://school.discoveryeducation.com

DLTK'S Educational Activities—http://www.dltk-teach.com

DyeTub Certificate Templates—http://www.dyetub.com/certificates/

Education World—http://www.education-world.com

EduHound—http://www.eduhound.com

Edutopia—http://www.edutopia.org

Enchanted Learning—http://www.enchantedlearning.com

Houghton Mifflin Harcourt Education Place—http://www.eduplace.com

Intervention Central—http://www.interventioncentral.org

Kathy Schrock's Guide for Educators—http://school.discovery.com/schrockguide/?pID=Kathy

Midlink Magazine—http://www.ncsu.edu/midlink/

PBS Teachers—http://www.pbs.org/teachers/

ProTeacher Community—http://www.proteacher.net

Scholastic—http://www.scholastic.com

Sites for Teachers—http://www.sitesforteachers.com

Starfall.com—http://www.starfall.com

Surfing the Net with Kids—http://www.surfnetkids.com

TeachersFirst.com—http://www.teachersfirst.com

Teachers.net—http://teachers.net

TeacherVision—http://www.teachervision.com

Teaching Ideas for Primary Teachers—http://www.teachingideas.co.uk

Teaching Tolerance—http://www.teachingtolerance.org

TeAchnology—http://www.teach-nology.com

Thinkfinity—http://www.marcopolo-education.org/home.aspx

Wikipedia: The Free Encyclopedia—http://www.wikipedia.org

Assessment Resources

AIMSweb—http://www.aimsweb.com

Alpine Achievement Systems—http://www.alpineachievement.com

Dynamic Indicators of Basic Early Literacy Skills (DIBELS)—http://dibels.uoregon.edu

Edcheckup—http://www.edcheckup.com

National Center on Student Progress Monitoring—http://www.student progress.org

Research Institute on Progress Monitoring—http://www.progress monitoring.net

Rubistar—http://rubistar.4teachers.org/index.php

Rubrics 4 Teachers—http://www.rubrics4teachers.com

Evidence-Based Practice Resources

Best Evidence Encyclopedia—http://www.bestevidence.org

The Campbell Collaboration—http://www.campbellcollaboration.org

Doing What Works—http://dww.ed.gov

Evidence for Policy and Practice Information and Co-ordinating Centre (EPPI-Centre)—http://www.eppi.ioe.ac.uk/cms/

What Works Clearinghouse—http://ies.ed.gov/ncee/wwc/

ESL Resources

Activities for Students—http://a4esl.org

Dave's Cafe—http://www.eslcafe.com

ESL Bears—http://eslbears.homestead.com

ESL Galaxy—http://www.esl-galaxy.com

ESL Resource Center—http://www.eslsite.com

Interesting Things for Students—http://www.manythings.org

National Association for Bilingual Education—http://www.nabe.org

National Clearinghouse for English Language Acquisition and Language Instructional Educational Programs (NCELA)—http://www.ncela.gwu.edu

Office of English Language Acquisition, Language Enhancement, and Academic Achievement for Limited English Proficient Students (OELA)—http://www.ed.gov/about/offices/list/oela/index.html

Teaching Diverse Learners—http://www.alliance.brown.edu/tdl/

Literacy Resources

Center for the Study of Reading—http://csr.ed.uiuc.edu

The Florida Center for Reading Research—http://www.fcrr.org

International Reading Association—http://www.reading.org

Literacy Matters—http://www.literacymatters.org

Oregon Reading First—http://oregonreadingfirst.uoregon.edu

Reading a-z.com—http://www.readinga-z.com/index.php

Vocabulary.com—http://www.vocabulary.com

Wordplays.com—http://www.wordplays.com

Wordsmith—http://wordsmith.org

Professional Resources

American Federation of Teachers—http://www.aft.org

Inspiring Teachers—http://www.inspiringteachers.com

Mid-continent Research for Education and Learning (McREL)—http://www.mcrel.org

National Board for Professional Teaching Standards—http://www.nbpts.org

National Center for Learning Disabilities—http://www.ld.org

National Comprehensive Center for Teacher Quality—http://www.tqsource.org

The National Council of Teachers of English—http://www.ncte.org

National Education Association (NEA)—http://www.nea.org

National Institute for Urban School Improvement—http://urban schools.org

National Staff Development Council—http://nsdc.org

New Horizons for Learning—http://www.newhorizons.org

Teachers Network—http://www.teachersnetwork.org/index.htm

Recognition & Response—http://www.recognitionandresponse.org

Teacher.com—http://www.teacher.com

Urban Special Education Leadership Collaborative—http://www.urban collaborative.org

U.S. Department of Education—http://www.ed.gov

Technology Resources

BestWebQuests—http://bestwebquests.com

CyberSleuth Kids—http://cybersleuth-kids.com

Filamentality—http://www.kn.pacbell.com/wired/fil/

Internet4Classrooms (I4C)—http://www.internet4classrooms.com/ on-line.htm

Online Internet Institute—http://oii.org

Quia Web—http://www.quia.com/web/

Web-and-Flow—http://www.web-and-flow.com

WebQuest.org—http://webquest.org

WebQuests for Learning—http://tommarch.com/learning/index.php

4Teachers.org—http://www.4teachers.org

Translation Resources

Babel Fish Translation—http://www.babelfish.yahoo.com

FreeTranslation.com—http://www.freetranslation.com

Language Dictionaries and Translators—http://www.word2word.com/ dictionary.html

Tower of English—http://towerofenglish.com

References and
Suggested Readings

Albrecht, K. (2006). *Social intelligence: The new science of success*. San Francisco: Jossey-Bass.

American Speech-Language-Hearing Association (ASHA) Joint Coordinating Committee on Evidence-Based Practice. (2005). *Evidence-based practice in communication disorders: Position statement*. Retrieved October 16, 2008, from http://www.asha.org/about/publications/leader-online/archives/2005/050524/f050524a4.htm

Amrein, A. L., & Berliner, D. C. (2003). The effects of high-stakes testing on student motivation and learning. *Educational Leadership, 60*(5), 32–38.

Anderson, L. W. (2004). *Increasing teacher effectiveness* (2nd ed.). Paris: UNESCO, International Institute for Educational Planning.

Anderson, L. W., Krathwohl, D. R., Airasian, P. W., Cruikshank, K. A., Mayer, R. E., Pintrich, et al. (Eds.). (2001). *A taxonomy for learning, teaching, and assessing: A revision of Bloom's taxonomy of educational objectives*. New York: Longman.

Anderson, L. W., & Walberg, J. J. (Eds.). (1993). *Time-piece: Extending and enhancing learning time*. Reston, VA: National Association of Secondary School Principals.

Argyle, M. (1999). Causes and correlates of happiness. In D. Kahneman, E. Diener, & N. Schwartz (Eds.), *Well-being: The foundations of hedonic psychology* (pp. 353–373). New York: Russell Sage Foundation.

Arnsten, A. F. T. (1998). The biology of being frazzled. *Science, 280*(5370), 1711–1712.

Baker, D., & Greenberg, C. (with Yalof, I.) (2007). *What happy women know: How new findings in positive psychology can change women's lives for the better*. New York: Rodale Books.

Barbetta, P. M., Norona, K. L., & Bicard, D. F. (2005). Classroom behavior management: A dozen common mistakes and what to do instead. *Preventing School Failure, 49*(3), 11–19.

Beck, I. L., McKeown, M. G., & Kucan, L. (2002). *Bringing words to life: Robust vocabulary instruction*. New York: Guilford Press.

Bender, Y. (2005). *The tactful teacher: Effective communication with parents, colleagues, and administrators*. White River Junction, VT: Nomad Press.

Billingsley, B. S. (2005). *Cultivating and keeping committed special education teachers: What principals and district leaders can do.* Thousand Oaks, CA: Corwin Press.

Blachowicz, L. Z., & Fisher, P. (2000). Vocabulary instruction. In M. L. Kamil, P. B. Mosenthal, P. D. Pearson, & R. Barr (Eds.), *Handbook of reading research* (Vol. 3., pp. 502–523). Mahwah, NJ: Lawrence Erlbaum.

Black, P., Harrison, C., Lee, C., Marshall, B., & William, D. (2004). Working inside the black box: Assessment for learning in the classroom. *Phi Delta Kappan, 86*(1), 8–21.

Black, P., & William, D. (1998). Assessment and classroom learning. *Assessment in Education, 5*(1), 7–71.

Blocher, D. H., Heppner, M., & Johnston, J. (2001). *Career planning for the 21st century* (2nd ed.). Denver, CO: Love.

Bloom, B. S., & Krathwohl, D. (1977). *Taxonomy of educational objectives: Handbook 1; Cognitive domain.* New York: Longman.

Bobek, B. L. (2002). Teacher resiliency: A key to career longevity. *The Clearing House, 75*(4), 202–205.

Borba, J. A., & Olvera, C. M. (2001). Student-led parent-teacher conferences. *The Clearing House, 74*(6), 333–336.

Borich, G. D., & Tombari, M. L. (1997). Educational psychology: A contemporary approach (2nd ed.). New York: Allyn & Bacon.

Bromley, K., Irwin-De Vitis, L., & Modlo, M. (1995). *Graphic organizers: Visual strategies for active learning.* New York: Scholastic Professional Books.

Brounstein, M. (2001). *Communicating effectively for dummies.* Hoboken, NJ: Wiley.

Caffarella, R. S. (2002). *Planning programs for adult learners: A practical guide for educators, trainers, and staff developers* (2nd ed.). San Francisco: Jossey-Bass.

Caine, R. N., & Caine, G. (1991). *Making connections: Teaching and the human brain.* Menlo Park, CA: Innovative Learning Publications.

Caine, R. N., Caine, G., McClintic, F., & Klimek, K. (2005). *The 12 brain/mind principles in action: The fieldbook for making connections, teaching, and the human brain.* Thousand Oaks, CA: Corwin Press.

Canfield, J., & Switzer, J. (2005). *The success principles: How to get from where you are to where you want to be.* New York: HarperCollins.

Carnevale, A. P., Gainer, L. J., & Meltzer, A. S. (1988). Workplace basics: The skills employers want. *Training & Development Journal, 42*, 22–26.

Carnine, D. (2000, April). *Why education experts resist effective practices (and what it would take to make education more like medicine).* Washington, DC: Thomas B. Fordham Foundation. (ERIC Document Reproduction Service No. ED442804)

Carter-Scott, C. (2000). *If success is a game, these are the rules: Ten rules for a fulfilling life.* New York: Broadway Books.

Cassady, J. C., & Johnson, R. E. (2002). Cognitive test anxiety and academic performance. *Contemporary Educational Psychology, 27*, 270–295.

The Center for Public Education. (2008). *School demographics: How many students with disabilities are in our schools?* Retrieved January 23, 2008, from http://www.centerforpubliceducation.org

CEO Forum on Education and Technology. (2001, June). *The CEO Forum school technology and readiness report: Key building blocks for student achievement in the*

21st century. Retrieved November 11, 2007, from http://www.ceoforum
.org/downloads/report4.pdf

Cerra, Cheli, & Jacoby, Ruth. (2005). *Teacher talk! The art of effective communication*. San Francisco: Jossey-Bass.

Chatterji, M. (2008). Synthesizing evidence from impact evaluations in education to inform action. *Educational Researcher, 37*(1), 23–26.

Cohen, L. G., & Spenciner, L. J. (2003). *Assessment of children and youth with special needs* (2nd ed.). Boston: Allyn & Bacon.

Covey, S. R. (2004). *The 7 habits of highly effective people: Powerful lessons in personal change* (15th anniversary ed.). New York: Free Press. (Original work published 1989)

Covey, S. R., Merrill, A. R., & Merrill, R. R. (1994). *First things first*. New York: Simon & Schuster.

Cradler, J., McNabb, M., Freeman, M., & Burchett, R. (2002). How does technology influence student learning? *Learning and Leading with Technology, 29*(8), 46–49, 56. Retrieved November 11, 2007, from http://caret.iste.org/caretadmin/resources_documents/29_8.pdf

Crawford, G. B. (2007). *Brain-based teaching with adolescent learning in mind* (2nd ed.). Thousand Oaks, CA: Corwin Press.

Crowley, K., & Elster, K. (2006). *Working with you is killing me: Freeing yourself from emotional traps at work*. New York: Warner Business Books.

The Dalai Lama. (2003). *The compassionate life*. Boston: Wisdom.

The Dalai Lama, & Cutler, H. C. (2003). *The art of happiness at work*. New York: Riverhead Press.

Daresh, J. C. (2003). *Teachers mentoring teachers: A practical approach to helping new and experienced staff*. Thousand Oaks, CA: Corwin Press.

Darling-Hammond, L. (2000). Teacher quality and student achievement: A review of state policy evidence. *Education Policy Analysis Archives, 8*(1). Retrieved September 27, 2007, from http://epaa.asu.edu/epaa/v8n1/

De Shazer, S. (1988). *Clues: Investigating solutions in brief therapy*. New York: W. W. Norton.

De Shazer, S. (1991). *Putting difference to work*. New York: W. W. Norton.

Deutsch, R. (2003, February 1). Battling teacher burnout. *Career News*. Retrieved January 12, 2007, from http://www2.edweek.org

Diamond, M., & Hopson, J. (1998). *Magic trees of the mind: How to nurture your child's intelligence, creativity, and healthy emotions from birth through adolescence*. New York: Penguin Books.

Dickward, N. (Ed.). (2003). The sustainability challenge: Taking edtech to the next level. Washington, DC: Benton Foundation. Retrieved November 11, 2007, from http://www.benton.org/publibrary/sustainability/sus_challenge.html

Dittmer, R. E. (2006). *151 quick ideas to manage your time*. Franklin Lakes, NJ: Career Press.

DivorceRate.org. (n.d.). *Divorce rate*. Retrieved February 10, 2008, from http://www.divorcerate.org

Doherty, W. J., & Carlson, B. Z. (2002). *Putting families first: Successful strategies for reclaiming family life in a hurry-up world*. New York: Henry Holt.

Dowd, K. O., & Liedtka, J. (1994). What corporations seek in MBA hires: A survey. *Selections, 10*(2), 34–39.

Drago, R. W. (2007). *Striking a balance: Work, family, life.* Boston: Economic Affairs Bureau.

Duffy, M. L., & Forgan, J. (2005). *Mentoring new special education teachers: A guide for mentors and program developers.* Thousand Oaks, CA: Corwin Press.

Durrant, M. (1995). *Creative strategies for school problems.* New York: Norton.

Dye, G. A., (2000). Graphic organizers to the rescue: Helping students link—and remember—information. *Teaching Exceptional Children, 32*(3), 72–76. Available October 16, 2008, at http://www.teachingld.org/pdf/teaching_how-tos/graphic_organizers.pdf

Echevarria, J., Vogt, M., & Short, D. J. (2004). *Making content comprehensible for English learners: The SIOP model* (2nd ed.). Boston: Pearson Education.

Education Commission of the States. (2004). *No Child Left Behind.* Retrieved November 1, 2007, from http://nclb2.ecs.org/Projects_Centers/index.aspx?issueid=gen&IssueName=General

Elias, M. J., & Arnold, H. (Eds.). (2006). *The educator's guide to emotional intelligence and academic achievement: Social-emotional learning in the classroom.* Thousand Oaks, CA: Corwin Press.

Elksnin, L. K., & Elksnin, N. (2006). *Teaching social-emotional skills at school and home.* Denver: Love.

Ellis, D. (1995). *Human being.* Rapid City, SD: Breakthrough Enterprises.

Ellis, D. (1998). *Life coaching: A new career for helping professionals.* Rapid City, SD: Breakthrough Enterprises.

Ellis, D. (2002). *Falling awake: Creating the life of your dreams.* Rapid City, SD: Breakthrough Enterprises. Available October 16, 2008, at http://www.fallingawake.com/falling-awake-book-toc.html

Emmer, E., Evertson, C. M., & Worsham, M. E. (2006). *Classroom management for middle and high school teachers* (7th ed.). Boston: Pearson Allyn & Bacon.

Etscheidt, S. K. (2006). Progress monitoring: Legal issues and recommendations for IEP teams. *Teaching Exceptional Children, 38*(3), 56–60.

Federal Interagency Forum on Child and Family Statistics. (2007). *America's children: Key national indicators of well-being, 2007.* Retrieved March 3, 2008, from http://childstats.gov/americaschildren/index.asp

Fletcher, K. L., & Bray, N. W. (1996). External memory strategy use in preschool children. *Merrill-Palmer Quarterly, 42,* 379–396.

Fralick, T. (2007). *Cultivating lasting happiness: A 7 step guide to mindfulness.* Eau Claire, WI: PESI.

Friend, M. P., & Bursuck, W. D. (2002). *Including students with special needs: A practical guide for classroom teachers.* Boston: Allyn & Bacon.

Friend, M. P., & Cook, L. (2007). *Interactions: Collaboration skills for school professionals.* Boston: Allyn & Bacon.

Fuchs, D., Fuchs, L. S., Mathes, P. G., & Simmons, D. C. (1997). Peer-assisted learning strategies: Making classrooms more responsive to diversity. *American Educational Research Journal, 34,* 174–206.

Fuchs, L. S., Fuchs, D., & Powell, S. (2004). *Using CBM for progress monitoring.* Washington, DC: American Institutes for Research (AIR).

Gardner, H. (1999). *Intelligence reframed: Multiple intelligences for the 21st century.* New York: Basic Books.

Gersten, R., Baker, S. K., Shanahan, T., Linan-Thompson, S., Collins, P., & Scarcella, R. (2007). *Effective literacy and English language instruction for English learners in the elementary grades: A practical guide* (NCEE 2007-4011). Washington, DC: National Center for Education Evaluation and Regional Assistance, Institute of Education Sciences, U.S. Department of Education.

Gettinger, M., & Seibert, J. K. (2002). Best practices in increasing academic learning time. In A. Thomas & J. Grimes (Eds.), *Best practices in school psychology IV* (pp. 773–787). Bethesda, MD: National Association of School Psychologists.

Gill, V. (2007). *The ten students you'll meet in your classroom: Classroom management tips for middle and high school teachers.* Thousand Oaks, CA: Corwin Press.

Goleman, D. (1995). *Emotional intelligence.* New York: Bantam Books.

Goleman, D. (1998). *Working with emotional intelligence.* New York: Bantam Books.

Goleman, D. (2006). *Social intelligence: The new science of human relationships.* New York: Bantam Books.

Gollnick, D. M., & Chinn, P. C. (2006). *Multicultural education in a pluralistic society* (7th ed.). Upper Saddle River, NJ: Pearson Prentice Hall.

Good, T. L., & Brophy, J. E. (2007). *Looking in classrooms* (10th ed.). New York: Longman.

Gottman, J. M., & Silver, N. (1999). *The seven principles for making marriage work: A practical guide from the country's foremost relationship expert.* New York: Crown.

Greenwood, C. R., Carta, J. J., & Hall, R. V. (1988). The use of peer tutoring strategies in classroom management and educational instruction. *School Psychology Review, 17,* 258–275.

Guthrie, J. T. (Ed.). (2008). *Engaging adolescents in reading.* Thousand Oaks, CA: Corwin Press.

Haddock, S., & Zimmerman, T. (2001). Ten adaptive strategies for family and work balance: Advice from successful families. *Journal of Marital and Family Therapy, 27*(4), 445–458.

Hall, K. A. (2006). *A life in balance: Nourishing the four roots of true happiness.* New York: AMACOM.

Hamre, B. K., & Pianta, R. C. (2005). Can instructional and emotional support in the first-grade classroom make a difference for children at risk for school failure? *Child Development, 76*(5), 949–967.

Harrington-Makin, D. (1994). *The team building tool kit.* New York: New Directions Management Services.

Hart, L. (1983). *Human brain, human learning.* New York: Longman.

Harvard Medical School. (2002). *Stress control.* Boston: Harvard Health.

Harvey, V. (2002). Best practices in teaching study skills. In A. Thomas & J. Grimes (Eds.), *Best practices in school psychology IV* (pp. 831–849). Bethesda, MD: National Association of School Psychologists.

Hattie, J., Biggs, J., & Purdie, N. (1996). Effects of learning skills interventions on student learning: A meta-analysis. *Review of Educational Research, 66,* 99–136.

Heafner, T. (2004). Using technology to motivate students to learn social studies. *Contemporary Issues in Technology and Teacher Education* (CITE), 4(1), 42–53. Retrieved November 11, 2007, from http://www.citejournal .org/articles/v4i1socialstudies1.pdf

Heron, T. E., Welsch, R. G., & Goddard, Y. L. (2003). Applications of tutoring systems in specialized subject areas: An analysis of skills, methodologies, and results. *Remedial and Special Education, 24,* 288–300.

Hewlitt, F., & Hewlitt, L. (2003). *The power of focus for women.* Deerfield Beach, FL: Health Communications.

Hohmann, M., & Weikart, D. P. (1995). *Educating young children.* Ypsilanti, MI: High/Scope Press.

Holloway, J. H. (2003). Addressing the needs of homeless students. *Educational Leadership, 60*(4), 89–90.

Hollowood, T. M., Salisbury, C. L., Rainforth, B., & Palombaro, M. M. (1995). Use of instructional time in classrooms serving students with and without severe disabilities. *Exceptional Children, 61,* 242–252.

Holmes, E. (2005). *Teacher well-being.* New York: RoutledgeFalmer.

Iran-Nejad, A. (1990). Active and dynamic self-regulation of learning processes. *Review of Educational Research, 60,* 573–602.

Jensen, E. (2006). *Enriching the brain: How to maximize every learner's potential.* San Francisco: Jossey-Bass.

Johnson, D. W., & Johnson, R. T. (1999). *Learning together and alone: Cooperative, competitive, and individualistic learning* (5th ed.). Boston: Allyn & Bacon.

Johnson, D. W., Johnson, R. T., & Holubec, E. (1993). *Cooperation in the classroom* (6th ed.). Edina, MN: Interaction Book.

John Wiley & Sons, Inc. (2008). *The Jossey-Bass reader on the brain and learning.* San Francisco: Author.

Joyce, B., & Showers, B. (1995). *Student achievement through staff development: Fundamentals of school renewal* (2nd ed.). White Plains, NY: Longman.

Kame'enui, E. J., Carnine, D. W., Dixon, R. C., Simmons, D. C., & Coyne, M. D. (2002). *Effective teaching strategies that accommodate diverse learners* (2nd ed.). Upper Saddle River, NJ: Merrill Prentice Hall.

Kelley, R. E. (1998). *How to be a star at work: 9 breakthrough strategies you need to succeed.* New York: Three Rivers Press.

Kelley, W. M. (2003). *Rookie teaching for dummies.* New York: Wiley.

Klem, A. M., & Connell, J. P. (2004). Relationships matter: Linking teacher support to students' engagement and achievement. *Journal of School Health, 74*(7), 262–273.

Kusche, C. A., & Greenberg, M. T. (2006). Brain development and social-emotional learning: An introduction for educators. In M. J. Elias and H. Arnold (Eds.). (2006). *The educator's guide to emotional intelligence and academic achievement: Social-emotional learning in the classroom* (pp. 15–34). Thousand Oaks, CA: Corwin Press.

Kyriakides, L., Campbell, R. J., & Christofidou, E. (2002). Generating criteria for measuring teacher effectiveness through a self-evaluation approach: A complementary way of measuring teacher effectiveness. *School Effectiveness and School Improvement, 13*(3), 291–325.

Lafasto, F., & Larson, C. (2001). *When teams work best.* Thousand Oaks, CA: Sage.

Lake, J., & Billingsly, B. (2000). An analysis of factors that contribute to parent-school conflict in special education. *Remedial and Special Education. 21*(4), 240–256.

Lane, K. L., Pierson, M. R., & Givner, C. C. (2003). Teacher expectations of student behavior: Which skills do elementary and secondary teachers deem necessary for success in the classroom? *Education and Treatment of Children, 26*(4), 413–430.

Langer, E. J. (2000). Mindful learning. *Current Directions in Psychological Science, 9,* 220–223.

Libbey, H. P. (2004). Measuring student relationships to school: Attachment, bonding, connectedness, and engagement. *Journal of School Health, 74*(7), 274–283.

Lipton, L., Wellman, B., & Humbard, C. (2003). *Mentoring matters: A practical guide to learning-focused relationships* (2nd ed.). Sherman, CT: Mira Via.

Lord Nelson, L. (2004, May/June). Boundaries in family-professional relationships. *Remedial and Special Education, 25*(3), 153–165.

Luckner, J. L. (2002). *Facilitating the transition of students who are deaf or hard of hearing.* Austin, TX: Pro-Ed.

Luckner, J. L., Bowen, S., & Carter, K. (2001). Visual teaching strategies for students who are deaf or hard of hearing. *Teaching Exceptional Children, 33*(3), 38–44.

Luckner, J. L., & Denzin, P. (1998). In the mainstream: Adaptations for students who are deaf or hard of hearing. *Perspectives in Education and Deafness, 17*(1), 8–11.

Luckner, J. L., & Nadler, R. S. (1997). *Processing the experience: Strategies to enhance and generalize learning* (2nd ed.). Dubuque, IA: Kendall/Hunt.

Mandel, S. (2007). *The parent-teacher partnership: How to work together for student achievement.* Chicago: Zephyr Press.

Martin J. A., Hamilton, B. E., Sutton, P. D., Ventura, S. J., Menacker, F., Kirmeyer, S., et al. (2007). Births: Final data for 2005. *National Vital Statistics Reports, 56*(6). Hyattsville, MD: National Center for Health Statistics. Retrieved October 16, 2008, from http://www.cdc.gov/nchs/fastats/unmarry.htm

Martin, K., & Brenny, K. (2005). *1000 best new teacher survival secrets: Face the classroom with confidence.* Naperville, IL: Sourcebooks.

Marzano, R. J. (2004). *Building background knowledge for academic achievement.* Alexandria, VA: Association for Supervision and Curriculum Development.

Maslow, A. H. (1987). *Motivation and personality* (3rd ed.). New York: Harper & Row.

Mastropieri, M. A., & Scruggs, T. E. (2000). *The inclusive classroom: Strategies for effective instruction.* Upper Saddle River, NJ: Prentice-Hall.

Mayo Clinic: Mayo Foundation for Medical Education and Research. (2006). *The Mayo Clinic plan: 10 essential steps to a better body and healthier life.* New York: Time.

McGraw, P. C. (1999). *Life strategies: Doing what works, doing what matters.* New York: Hyperion.

Mehrabian, A. (1980). *Silent messages* (2nd ed). Belmont, CA: Wadsworth.

Meisels, S. J., Atkins-Burnett, S., Xue, Y., & Bickel, D. P. (2003). Creating a system of accountability: The impact of instructional assessment on elementary children's achievement test scores. *Educational Policy Analysis Archives, 11*(9), 1–19.

Merriam-Webster's Collegiate Dictionary (11th ed.). (2006). Springfield, MA: Merriam-Webster.

Montgomery, W. (2001). Creating culturally responsive, inclusive classrooms. *Teaching Exceptional Children, 33*(4), 4–9.

Morgan, G. A., Harmon, R. J., & Maslin-Cole, C. A. (1990). Mastery motivation: Definition and measurement. *Early Education and Development, 1*(5), 318–339.

Mroczek, D. (1999). Lessons in happiness from a major American study on happiness. *Bottom Line Personal, 20*(2), 13–14.

Myers, D. G. (2000). The funds, friends, and faith of happy people. *American Psychologist, 55*(1), 56–67.

Nadler, R. S. (2007). *Leaders' playbook.* Santa Barbara, CA: Psycess Press.

Nastasi, B. K., & Clements, D. H. (1991). Research on cooperative learning: Implications for practice. *School Psychology Review, 20,* 110–131.

National Center for Education Statistics. (2007). *Status and trends in the education of racial and ethnic minorities.* Jessup, MD: U.S. Department of Education. National Clearinghouse for English Language Acquisition and Language Instruction Educational Programs (NCELA). (2006). *The growing numbers of limited English proficient students: 1995/96–2005/06* [Poster]. Retrieved February 2, 2008 from http://www.ncela.gwu.edu/stats/2_nation.htm

National PTA. (1998). *National standards for parent/family involvement programs.* Chicago: Author. Retrieved October 16, 2008, from http://www.pta.org/Documents/National_Standards.pdf

National Sleep Foundation. (2005, March). *2005 sleep in America poll.* Washington, D.C.: Author.

No Child Left Behind Act of 2001, 20 U.S.C. §§ 6301 *et seq.* (2002)

Norton, P., & Sprague, D. (2001). *Technology in teaching.* Boston: Allyn & Bacon.

Ogle, D. M. (1986). K-W-L: A teaching model that develops active reading of expository text. *The Reading Teacher, 39,* 564–570.

Organization for Economic Co-operation and Development (OECD). (2007). *Education at a glance 2007: OECD indicators.* Retrieved February 15, 2008, from http://www.oecd.org/dataoecd/36/4/40701218.pdf

Ormrod, J. E. (2008). *Human learning* (5th ed.). Upper Saddle River, NJ: Pearson Education.

Panel on Education Technology. (1997, March). *Report to the president on the use of technology to strengthen K–12 education in the United States.* Washington, DC: President's Committee of Advisors on Science and Technology. Available October 16, 2008, at http://www.ostp.gov/cs/report_to_the_president_on_the_use_of_technology_to_strengthen_k12_education_in_the_united_states

Park, J., Turnbull, A. P., & Turnbull, H. R. (2002). Impacts of poverty on quality of life in families of children with disabilities. *Exceptional Children, 68,* 151–172.

Pashler, H., Bain, P., Bottge, B., Graesser, A., Koedinger, K., McDaniel, M., et al. (2007). *Organizing instruction and study to improve student learning* (NCER 2007–2004). Washington, DC: National Center for Education Research, Institute of Education Sciences, U.S. Department of Education.

Petreshene, S. S. (1985). *Mind joggers: 5- to 15-minute activities that make kids think.* West Nyack, NY: Center for Applied Research in Education (CARE).

Polloway, E. A., Patton, J. R., & Serna, L. (2005). *Strategies for teaching learners with special needs* (8th ed.). Upper Saddle River, NJ: Pearson Education.

Pomerantz, E. M., Moorman, E. A., & Litwack, S. D. (2007). The how, whom and why of parents' involvement in children's academic lives: More is not always better. *Review of Education Research, 77*(3), 373–410.

Popham, W. J. (2003). *Test better, teach better: The instructional role of assessment.* Alexandria, VA: Association for Supervision and Curriculum Development.

Pressley, M., Woloshyn, V., Burkell, J., Cariglia-Bull, T., Lysynchuk, L., McGoldrick, J. A., et al. (1995). *Cognitive strategy instruction that really improves children's academic performance.* Cambridge, MA: Brookline.

Pugach, M. C., & Johnson, L. L. (2002). *Collaborative practitioners, collaborative schools* (2nd ed.). Denver, CO: Love.

Purkey, W. W., & Novak, J. M. (1984). *Inviting school success: A self-concept approach to teaching and learning* (2nd ed.). Belmont, CA: Wadsworth.

Putnam, J. W. (Ed.) (1998). *Cooperative learning and strategies for inclusion* (2nd ed.). Baltimore: Paul H. Brookes.

Rath, T. (2006). *Vital friends.* New York: Gallup Press.

Rath, T., & Clifton, D. O. (2004). How full is your bucket? Positive strategies for work and life. New York: Gallup Press.

Rauch, M., & Fillenworth, C. (1995). Motivating students to use newly learned study strategies. *Journal of Reading, 38,* 567–568.

Resnick, L. B. (1987). *Education and learning to think.* Washington, DC: National Academy Press.

Reutzel, D. R., & Cooter, R. B. (2000). *Teaching children to read* (3rd ed.). Upper Saddle River, NJ: Merrill.

Richards, H. V., Brown, A. F., & Forde, T. B. (2007). Addressing diversity in schools: Culturally responsive pedagogy. *Teaching Exceptional Children, 39,* 64–68.

Richardson, C. (1999). *Take time for your life.* New York: Broadway Books.

Richardson, C. (2002). *Stand up for your life: A practical step-by-step plan to build inner confidence and personal power.* New York: Free Press.

Rogers, C. R. (1961). *On becoming a person: A therapist's view of psychotherapy.* Boston: Houghton Mifflin.

Rohrbeck, C. A., Ginsburg-Block, M. D., Fantuzzo, J. W., & Miller, T. R. (2003). Peer-assisted learning interventions with elementary students: A meta-analytic review. *Journal of Educational Psychology, 95,* 240–257.

Rose, D. H., Meyer, A., Strangman, N., & Rappolt, G. (2002). *Teaching every student in the digital age: Universal design for learning.* Alexandria, VA: Association for Supervision and Curriculum Development.

Rosenberg, M. (2003). *Nonviolent communication.* Encinitas, CA: Puddle Dancer Press.

Rosenshine, B. V. (1986). Synthesis of research on explicit teaching. *Educational Leadership, 43*(7), 60–69.

Ruiz-de-Velasco, J., & Fix, M. (2000). *Overlooked and underserved: Immigrant students in U.S. secondary schools.* Washington, DC: Urban Institute.

Ryan, R. M., & Deci, E. L. (2000). Self-determination theory and the facilitation of intrinsic motivation, social development, and well-being. *American Psychologist, 55*(1), 68–78.

Saenz, L. M., Fuchs, L. S., & Fuchs, D. (2005). Peer-assisted learning strategies for English language learners with learning disabilities. *Exceptional Children, 71,* 231–247.

Salvia, J., & Ysseldyke, J. E. (with Bolt, S.). (2006). *Assessment in special and inclusive education* (10th ed.). Boston: Thomson Wadsworth.

Scruggs, T. E., & Mastropieri, M. A. (1992). *Teaching test-taking skills: Helping students show what they know.* Cambridge, MA: Brookline.

Secretary's Commission on Achieving Necessary Skills. (1991). *What work requires of schools: A SCANS Report for America 2000.* Washington, DC: U.S. Department of Labor. Available October 16, 2008, at http://wdr.doleta.gov/SCANS/whatwork/

Seidel, T., & Shavelson, R. J. (2007). Teaching effectiveness research in the past decade: The role of theory and research design in disentangling meta-analysis results. *Review of Educational Research, 77*(4), 454–499.

Selekman, M. (1993). *Pathways to change.* New York: Guilford Press.

Seligman, M. E. P. (2002). *Authentic happiness: Using the new positive psychology to realize your potential for lasting fulfillment.* New York: Free Press.

Seligman, M. E. P., & Csikszentmihalyi, M. (2000). Positive psychology: An introduction. *American Psychologist, 55*(1), 5–14.

Senge, P. (2000). *Schools that learn.* New York: Doubleday Dell.

Shalaway, L. (1998). *Learning to teach.* New York: Scholastic Professional Books.

Siegler, R. S., & Alibali, M. W. (2005). *Children's thinking* (4th ed.). Upper Saddle River, NJ: Pearson Prentice Hall.

Silberman, M. (1996). *Active learning: 101 strategies to teach any subject.* Boston: Allyn & Bacon.

Slavin, R. E. (1995). *Cooperative learning: Theory, research, and practice* (2nd ed.). Boston: Allyn & Bacon.

Smith, T. W. (2007, April). *Job satisfaction in the United States.* Chicago: National Opinion Research Center (NORC), University of Chicago. Retrieved January 2, 2008, from http://www.norc.org/publications/satisfaction.htm

Snell, M. E., & Janney, R. (2000). *Social relationships and peer support.* Baltimore: Paul H. Brookes.

Sousa, D. A. (2001). *How the brain learns* (2nd ed.). Thousand Oaks, CA: Corwin Press.

Stiggins, R. J. (2005). *Student-involved assessment FOR learning* (4th ed.). Upper Saddle River, NJ: Pearson Prentice Hall.

Stronge, J. H. (2002). *Qualities of effective teachers.* Alexandria, VA: Association for Supervision and Curriculum Development.

Stronge, J. H., & Hindman, J. L. (2003). Hiring the best teachers. *Educational Leadership, 60*(8), 48–52.

Tarquin, P., & Walker, S. (1997). *Creating success in the classroom: Visual organizers and how to use them.* Englewood, CO: Teacher Ideas Press.

Taulbert, C. L. (2006). *Eight habits of the heart for educators: Building strong school communities through timeless values.* Thousand Oaks, CA: Corwin Press.

Taylor, S. E., Kemeny, M., Reed, G. M., Bower, J. E., & Gruenewald, T. L. (2000). Psychological resources, positive illusions, and health. *American Psychologist, 55*(1), 99–109.

Thompson, J. G. (2007). *The first-year teacher's survival guide: Ready to use strategies, tools & activities for meeting the challenges of each school day* (2nd ed.). San Francisco: John Wiley & Sons.

Thorsen, C. (2003). *TechTactics: Instructional models for educational computing.* Boston: Allyn & Bacon.

Tobin, K. (1987). The role of wait time in higher cognitive level learning. *Review of Educational Research, 57,* 69–95.

Todd, K. W., & McNergney, R. F. (1999). *Will technology really change education? From blackboard to Web.* Thousand Oaks, CA: Corwin Press.

Tomlinson, C. A. (2005). *The differentiated classroom: Responding to the needs of all learners.* Upper Saddle River, NJ: Pearson Education.

Tovani, C. (2004). *Do I really have to teach reading? Content comprehension grades 6–12.* Portland, ME: Stenhouse.

Tracy, B. (1993). *Action strategies for personal achievement.* Niles, IL: Nightingale-Conant.

Trumbull, E., & Pacheco, M. (2005). *Leading with diversity: Cultural competencies for teacher preparation and professional development.* Providence, RI: Brown University.

Tuckman, B. W., & Jensen, M. A. (1977). Stages of small group development revisited. *Group and Organizational Studies, 2,* 419–427.

Turnbull, A., & Turnbull, R. (2001). *Families, professionals, and exceptionality: Collaborating for power* (4th ed.). Upper Saddle River, NJ: Merrill Prentice-Hall.

U.S. Census Bureau. (2006). Fact Sheet: United States 2006. In *American FactFinder.* Retrieved February 10, 2008, from http://factfinder.census.gov/servlet/ACSSAFFFacts

U.S. Census Bureau. (2007a). *Minority population tops 100 million.* Retrieved October 3, 2007, from http://www.census.gov/Press-Release/www/releases/archives/population/010048.html

U.S. Census Bureau. (2007b). *Poverty: 2006 highlights.* Retrieved May 16, 2008, from http://www.census.gov/hhes/www/poverty/poverty06/pov06hi.html

U.S. Department of Education Institute of Education Sciences. (2007). *Digest of education statistics: 2007.* Retrieved October 16, 2008, from http://nces.ed.gov/programs/digest/d07/

U.S. Equal Opportunity Commission. (2002). *Sexual harassment.* Retrieved June 20, 2008, from http://eeoc.gov/facts/fs-sex.html

Vaughn, S., Bos, C. S., & Schumm, J. S. (2007). *Teaching students who are exceptional, diverse, and at risk in the general education classroom* (4th ed.). Boston: Pearson Education.

Warrell, M. (2007). *Find your courage! Unleash your full potential and live the life you really want.* Austin, TX: Synergy Books.

Wayne, A. J., & Youngs, P. (2003). Teacher characteristics and student achievement gains: A review. *Review of Educational Research, 73*(1), 89–122.

White, M., & Dorman, S. M. (2000). De-densify information overload. *The Education Digest, 66*(1), 27–30.

Wiggins, G., & McTighe, J. (1998). *Understanding by design.* Upper Saddle River, NJ: Prentice-Hall.

Workplace Bullying Institute. (2007). *U.S. workplace bullying survey.* Retrieved June 20, 2008, from http://bullyinginstitute.org/wbi-zogby2007.html

Wormeli, R. (2007). *Differentiation: From planning to practice grades 6–12.* Portland, ME: Stenhouse.

Zimmerman, T., Haddock, S., Ziemba, S., & Rust, A. (2001). Family organizational labor: Who's calling the plays? *Journal of Feminist Family Therapy, 13*(2/3), 65–90.

Index

CORWIN

A SAGE Company

The Corwin logo—a raven striding across an open book—represents the union of courage and learning. Corwin is committed to improving education for all learners by publishing books and other professional development resources for those serving the field of PreK–12 education. By providing practical, hands-on materials, Corwin continues to carry out the promise of its motto: **"Helping Educators Do Their Work Better."**